Oxford Picture Dictionary of American English

French Indexed Edition

E. C. PARNWELL

ILLUSTRATED BY
BERNARD CASE
CORINNE CLARKE
RAY BURROWS

FRENCH LINGUISTIC CONSULTANTS
JACQUELINE STRATFORD
ALISON D'ANGLEJAN

New York   OXFORD UNIVERSITY PRESS   1978

©1978 by Oxford University Press, Inc.

Library of Congress Cataloging in Publication Data

Parnwell, E. C.
Oxford picture dictionary of American English.
Includes index.
SUMMARY: Teaches English as a second language
to French speakers through the use of pictures
dealing with everyday topics such as the body,
post office, law, travel, and family.
1. English language in the United States.
2. Picture dictionaries, English. 3. English
language—Text-books for foreigners—French.
I. Case, Bernard. II. Clarke, Corinne.
III. Burrows, Ray. IV. Title.
PE2835.P33   423   77-18463   ISBN 0-19-502334-X

Notes from the English Language Teaching Department

We are proud to present the first contextualized Oxford Picture Dictionary using American English. This dictionary can be used for communicative purposes. It will stimulate exciting conversations about everyday topics which students come in contact with. It can also be used as a handy reference for students studying on their own.

We hope you enjoy using this dictionary. We welcome your comments as always.

MANAGER: Marilyn S. Rosenthal, Ph.D.
EDUCATIONAL SPECIALIST: Connie Attanasio, M.A.
EDITOR: Laurie Likoff, M.A.

Fifth printing, 1980

Printed in the United States of America

CONTENTS

A.   In Space
1   comet
2   constellation
3   galaxy
4   planet
5   star
6   Moon
7   Earth
8   Sun
9   orbit

B.   Phases of the Moon
10   eclipse

11   new/crescent moon
12   half moon
13   full moon
14   old moon

C.   Space Travel
15   nosecone
16   rocket
17   launch(ing) pad
18   satellite
19   (space) capsule
20   astronaut
21   spacesuit

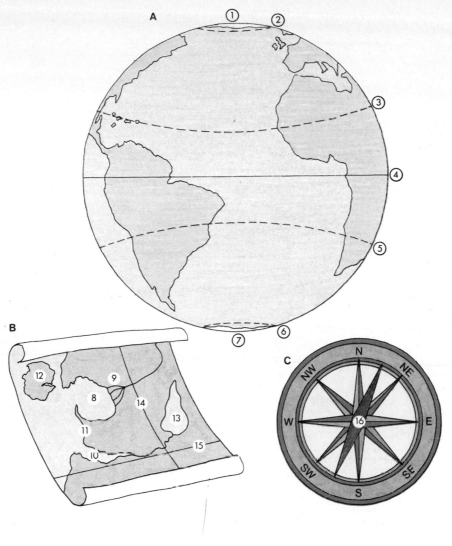

A. Globe
1 North Pole
2 Arctic Circle
3 Tropic of Cancer
4 Equator
5 Tropic of Capricorn
6 Antarctic Circle
7 South Pole

B. Map
8 bay
9 delta
10 estuary
11 coastline
12 island

13 lake
14 line of longitude
15 line of latitude

C. Compass
16 needle
N   north
NE   northeast
E   east
SE   southeast
S   south
SW   southwest
W   west
NW   northwest

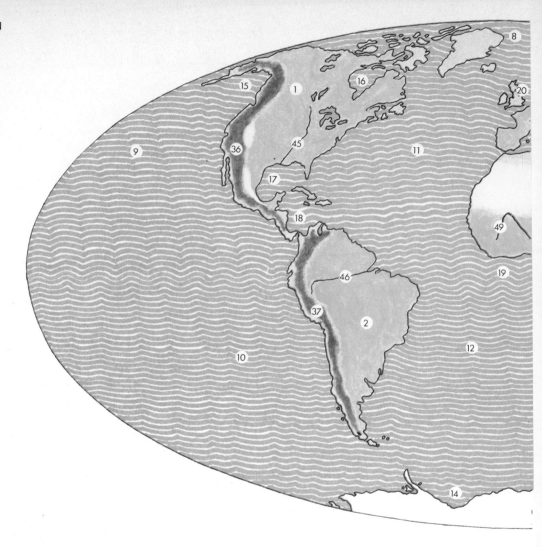

Continents
1   North America
2   South America
3   Europe
4   Africa
5   Asia
6   Australia
7   Antarctica

Oceans
8   Arctic
9   North Pacific
10   South Pacific
11   North Atlantic
12   South Atlantic
13   Indian
14   Southern

Seas, Gulfs, Bays
15   Gulf of Alaska
16   Hudson Bay
17   Gulf of Mexico
18   Caribbean Sea
19   Gulf of Guinea
20   North Sea
21   Baltic Sea
22   Mediterranean Sea
23   Black Sea
24   Caspian Sea
25   Red Sea
26   Persian Gulf
27   Arabian Sea
28   Bay of Bengal
29   Coral Sea
30   Tasman Sea

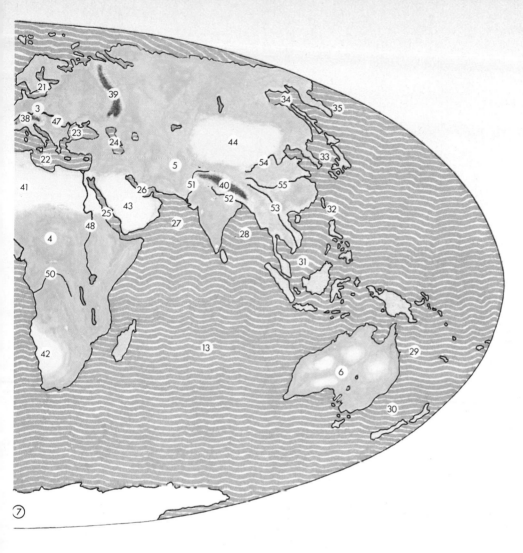

31	South China Sea	43	Arabian
32	East China Sea	44	Gobi
33	Sea of Japan		
34	Sea of Okhotsk		
35	Bering Sea		

Rivers

45 Mississippi

Mountain Ranges

46 Amazon

36 Rockies

47 Danube

37 Andes

48 Nile

38 Alps

49 Niger

39 Urals

50 Congo

40 Himalayas

51 Indus

52 Ganges

Deserts

53 Mekong

41 Sahara

54 Yellow

42 Kalahari

55 Yangtze

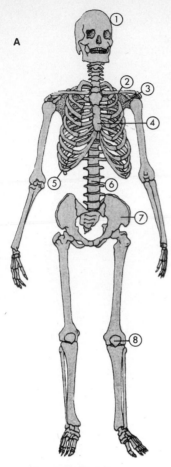

A

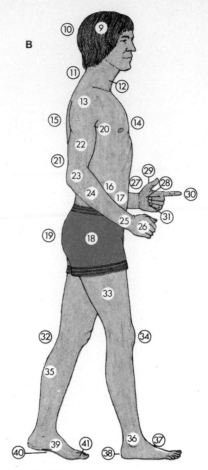

B

A.	**The Skeleton**	18	hip
1	skull	19	buttocks
2	collar bone	20	armpit
3	shoulder blade	21	arm
4	breastbone	22	upper arm
5	rib	23	elbow
6	backbone/spine	24	forearm
7	hip bone/pelvis	25	wrist
8	kneecap	26	fist
		27	hand
B.	**The Body**	28	palm
9	hair	29	thumb
10	head	30	finger
11	neck	31	nail/fingernail
12	throat	32	leg
13	shoulder	33	thigh
14	chest	34	knee
15	back	35	calf
16	waist	36	ankle
17	stomach	37	foot

C

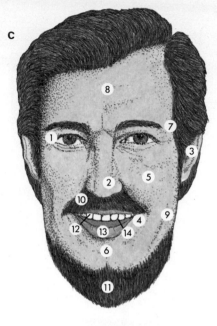

D

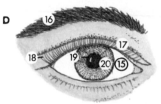

E

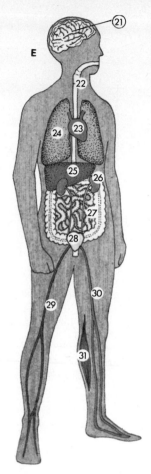

38 heel	**D. The Eye**
39 instep	15 eyeball
40 sole	16 eyebrow
41 toe	17 eyelid
	18 eyelashes
	19 pupil
C. The Face	20 iris
1 eye	
2 nose	**E. The Insides**
3 ear	21 brain
4 mouth	22 windpipe
5 cheek	23 heart
6 chin	24 lung
7 temple	25 liver
8 forehead	26 kidney
9 jaw	27 intestines
10 mustache	28 bladder
11 beard	29 vein
12 tooth	30 artery
13 lip	31 muscle
14 tongue	

1	bathrobe	11	shoe
2	pajamas	12	rubber boot
3	slipper	13	sneaker/tennis shoe
4	undershirt/T-shirt	14	jeans
5	(under)shorts	15	sweater
6	sock	16	belt
7	jacket/sport coat	17	buckle
8	slacks	18	boot
9	(cardigan) sweater	19	jacket
10	loafer		

1	shirt	16	pocket
2	collar	17	trousers/pants
3	cuff	18	cuff
4	tie	19	scarf
5	vest	20	glove
6	suit	21	watch
7	sleeve	22	watchband
8	shoe	23	glasses
9	shoelace	24	umbrella
10	sole	25	cuff links
11	heel	26	button
12	trenchcoat/raincoat	27	jacket/sport coat
13	hat	28	briefcase
14	overcoat/coat	29	slacks
15	lapel	30	rain hat

1	bra	13	mascara
2	slip	14	nail polish
3	panties	15	perfume
4	panty hose	16	eye shadow
5	nightgown	17	face cream
6	slipper	18	lipstick
7	ring	19	comb
8	bracelet	20	brush
9	earring	21	bathrobe
10	necklace	22	roller
11	nail file	23	clip
12	compact		

1 turtleneck sweater	10 dress
2 pantsuit	11 coat
3 boot	12 (knee) sock
4 (shoulder) bag / purse	13 barrette
5 suit	14 jeans
6 blouse	15 shirt
7 (suit) jacket	16 sweater
8 skirt	17 sandal
9 handkerchief	

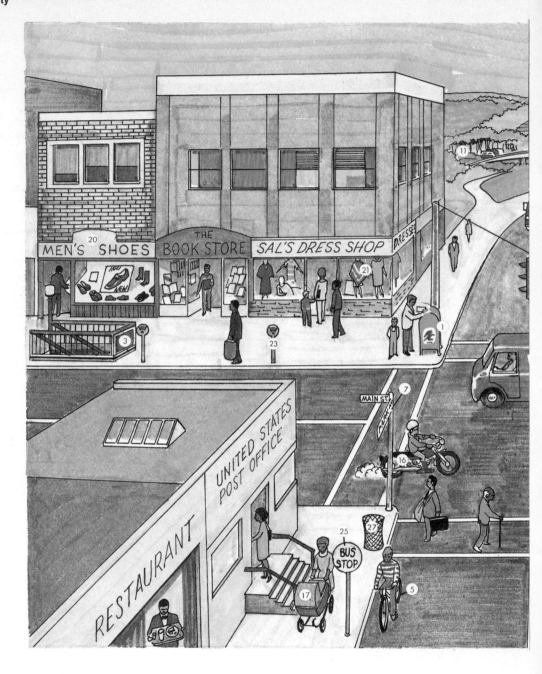

1	mailbox	9	gutter
2	crosswalk	10	drain/sewer
3	subway station	11	park
4	taxi/taxicab	12	bridge
5	bicycle	13	van
6	traffic light	14	truck
7	street sign	15	intersection
8	curb	16	motorcycle

17	baby carriage	25	bus stop
18	apartment house	26	sidewalk
19	office building	27	trash can
20	store	28	telephone booth
21	display window	29	parking lot
22	street light	30	car
23	parking meter	31	street/road
24	bus		

A.

B.

C.

A.   Fire Department
1   fireman
2   fireman's hat
3   (fire) hose
4   (fire) hydrant
5   fire extinguisher
6   (fireman's) boot
7   fire engine
8   ladder
9   nozzle
10   bell
11   fire escape
12   fire
13   smoke

B.   At the Dentist
14   dental assistant
15   dentist's chair
16   dentist
17   drill
18   lamp/light

C.   A Hospital Ward
19   (hospital) bed
20   patient
21   doctor
22   stethoscope
23   sling
24   X-ray
25   nurse
26   crutches
27   bandage

1 teacher	11 compass
2 blackboard	12 protractor
3 eraser	13 glue
4 chalk	14 book
5 student	15 notebook
6 book bag	16 slide rule
7 desk	17 loose-leaf paper
8 pencil	18 loose-leaf notebook
9 pen	19 map
10 ruler	20 calendar

1	scales	12	Bunsen burner
2	pan	13	tripod
3	weights	14	rubber tubing
4	meter	15	beaker
5	dial	16	flask
6	needle/pointer	17	crystals
7	bench	18	pipette
8	stool	19	magnet
9	microscope	20	pestle
10	lens	21	mortar
11	slide	22	test tube

1	shopping cart	15	shelf
2	cashier	16	canned food
3	cash register	17	fruit
4	checkout counter	18	vegetables
5	customer	19	bread
6	sack/bag	20	cookies
7	(shopping) basket	21	cake
8	clerk	22	fish
9	cheese	23	receipt
10	milk	24	bills
11	eggs	25	coins
12	hot dogs	26	crackers
13	meat	27	potatoes
14	freezer	28	soap powder

1 desk	15 switchboard
2 telephone	16 operator
3 calculator	17 calendar
4 blotter	18 file
5 appointment book	19 file/filing cabinet
6 hole puncher	20 carbon paper
7 stapler	21 typewriter
8 adding machine	22 secretary
9 paper clip	23 steno pad
10 bulletin board	24 bookcase
11 envelope	25 receptionist
12 in-box	26 card file
13 wastepaper basket	27 pencil holder
14 photocopier	

1 postal clerk	12 return address
2 scale	13 zip code
3 counter	14 postcard
4 mailbox	15 envelope
5 mailman	16 flap
6 mailbag	17 telegram/cable
7 aerogram	18 money order
8 postmark	19 package
9 stamp	20 string
10 (airmail) envelope	21 label
11 address	

1	crane	13	shovel
2	bricklayer	14	workman
3	rafters	15	sand
4	shingle	16	cement
5	ladder	17	trowel
6	rung	18	hod
7	scaffolding	19	level
8	bricks	20	excavator
9	drainpipe	21	cement mixer
10	foundations	22	dump truck
11	board	23	pneumatic drill
12	pick(ax)	24	wheelbarrow

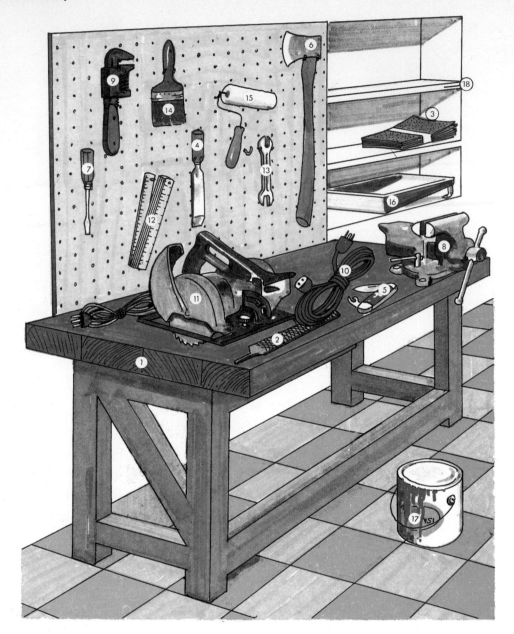

1	workbench	10	extension cord
2	file	11	power saw
3	sandpaper	12	folding rule
4	chisel	13	wrench
5	pocket knife	14	paintbrush
6	axe	15	(paint) roller
7	screwdriver	16	(paint) pan
8	vise	17	paint can
9	monkey wrench	18	shelf

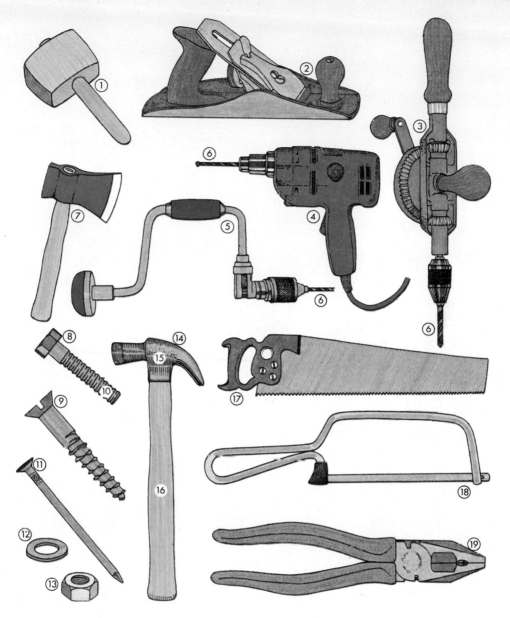

1 mallet	11 nail
2 plane	12 washer
3 hand drill	13 nut
4 electric drill	14 hammer
5 brace	15 head
6 bit	16 handle
7 hatchet	17 saw
8 bolt	18 hacksaw
9 screw	19 pliers
10 thread	

1 roof	12 shutter
2 chimney	13 window box
3 (outside) wall	14 curtain
4 balcony	15 blind
5 patio	16 gutter
6 garage	17 drainpipe
7 (front) door	18 doormat
8 window	19 antenna/aerial
9 window frame	20 (tool) shed
10 windowpane	21 grass
11 (window)sill	

The Weather
1   lightning
2   (storm)cloud
3   rain
4   raindrops
5   snow
6   snowball
7   snowman
8   icicle
9   sun
10   sky

In the Yard
11   tree
12   trunk
13   branch
14   twigs

15   leaves
16   gate
17   hedge
18   path
19   lawn
20   flower
21   flower bed
22   bush
23   watering can
24   flower pot
25   pitchfork
26   shed
27   wheelbarrow
28   clothesline
29   laundry
30   clothespin

1	door	12	staircase
2	mail slot	13	banister
3	lock and chain	14	upstairs
4	bolt	15	downstairs
5	hinge	16	light
6	(door)mat	17	(light) switch
7	floor	18	telephone/phone
8	rug	19	receiver
9	(coat)rack	20	dial
10	hook	21	cord
11	stair	22	telephone book

1	ceiling	16	bookcase
2	wall	17	shelf
3	carpet	18	amplifier
4	fireplace	19	turntable
5	mantel	20	speaker
6	fire	21	record
7	curtain	22	(record) jacket
8	drape	23	coffee table
9	couch/sofa	24	radio
10	cushion	25	end table
11	armchair	26	lamp
12	newspaper	27	lampshade
13	chair	28	television/TV
14	magazine rack	29	ashtray
15	magazine		

1	stove	21	can opener
2	oven	22	can
3	broiler	23	bottle opener
4	burner	24	dishwasher
5	refrigerator	25	dish towel
6	cabinet	26	table
7	sink	27	chair
8	counter	28	napkin
9	garbage can	29	napkin holder
10	fruit basket	30	place mat
11	fruit	31	knife
12	pot	32	spoon
13	pan	33	fork
14	skillet/frying pan	34	plate
15	bread box	35	bowl
16	shelf	36	glass
17	(tea) kettle	37	cup
18	toaster	38	sugar bowl
19	electric can opener	39	saltshaker
20	coffee pot	40	pepper shaker

1	vacuum cleaner	11	iron
2	broom	12	cord
3	ironing board	13	(light)bulb
4	washing machine	14	hair dryer
5	mop	15	plug
6	dust brush	16	outlet/socket
7	dustcloth	17	switch
8	dustpan	18	soap powder
9	scouring powder	19	pail/bucket
10	scrub brush		

The Bedroom

1   bed
2   headboard
3   pillow
4   pillowcase
5   sheet
6   blanket
7   bedspread
8   mattress
9   night table
10 dressing table
11 dressing table skirt
12 stool
13 mirror
14 closet
15 desk
16 chest of drawers
17 rug
18 toy box
19 toy
20 game
21 hair brush
22 comb
23 box of tissues
24 jewelry box
25 alarm clock

The Baby

26 crib
27 sleeper
28 pacifier
29 stuffed animal
30 rattle
31 doll
32 changing table
33 bottle
34 nipple
35 bib
36 diaper
37 baby powder

1	bathtub/tub	17	toothbrush
2	hot water faucet	18	glass
3	cold water faucet	19	washcloth
4	shower head	20	nail brush
5	drain	21	toothpaste
6	drain plug	22	towel
7	diverter	23	towel rack
8	toilet	24	(bathroom) scale
9	handle	25	bath mat
10	toilet paper	26	sponge
11	medicine chest	27	soap
12	sink	28	hamper
13	razor	29	tile
14	(razor) blade	30	curtain rod
15	shaving mug	31	shower curtain
16	shaving brush		

1	plateau	11	meadow
2	mountain	12	river
3	(mountain) peak	13	field
4	waterfall	14	hedge
5	lake	15	tree
6	valley	16	village
7	stream	17	(foot)path
8	wood	18	road
9	forest	19	pond
10	hill		

1 tent	20 bathing trunks
2 groundcloth	21 flipper
3 sleeping bag	22 sand
4 backpack	23 sandcastle
5 camp(ing) stove	24 bucket
6 cliff	25 shovel
7 hotel	26 beach ball
8 cottage	27 seashell
9 boardwalk	28 pebbles
10 seawall	29 rocks
11 beach	30 kite
12 beach umbrella	31 water
13 sunbather	32 surf
14 (beach) towel	33 wave
15 mask/goggles	34 motorboat
16 snorkel	35 swimmer
17 ice cream	36 bathing suit
18 windbreaker	37 seaweed
19 deck chair	

1	hayloft	19	plow
2	hay	20	furrow
3	cow shed	21	cow
4	barn	22	calf
5	pen	23	bull
6	barnyard	24	goats
7	farm house	25	horse
8	field	26	mane
9	pond	27	hoof
10	fence	28	saddle
11	fruit tree	29	sheep
12	orchard	30	lamb
13	scarecrow	31	duckling
14	wheat	32	duck
15	farmer	33	hen/chicken
16	combine	34	rooster
17	irrigation canal	35	chick
18	tractor		

1 reservoir	8 cooling tower
2 dam	9 coal
3 powerhouse	10 derrick
4 cable	11 oil-rig
5 pylon	12 pipeline
6 power station	13 refinery
7 smokestack	14 storage tank

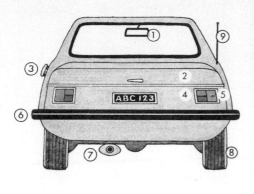

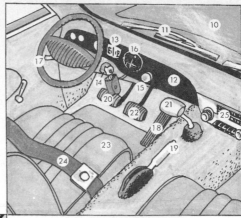

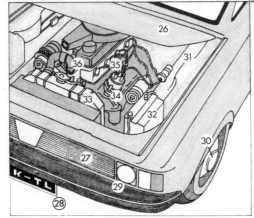

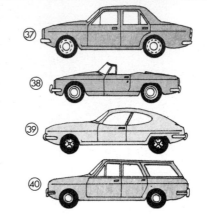

The Car

1	rearview mirror	21	gearshift
2	trunk	22	brake
3	gas cap	23	seat
4	taillight	24	seat/safety belt
5	turn signal	25	car radio
6	bumper	26	hood
7	exhaust	27	grill
8	tire	28	license plate
9	antenna/aerial	29	headlight
10	windshield	30	hubcap
11	windshield wiper	31	engine
12	dashboard	32	battery
13	fuel/gas gauge	33	radiator
14	ignition	34	distributor
15	choke	35	spark plug
16	speedometer	36	cylinder head
17	steering wheel	37	sedan
18	accelerator	38	convertible
19	hand/emergency brake	39	sports coupe
20	clutch	40	station wagon

1	thruway/freeway/expressway	12	transporter
2	overpass	13	trailer
3	underpass	14	truck
4	circle	15	ambulance
5	left/outside lane	16	car
6	right/inside lane	17	bus
7	gas station	18	sports car
8	gas pump	19	oil truck
9	air pump	20	motorcycle
10	attendant	21	trailer
11	trailer truck	22	van

1	bicycle/bike	20	reflector
2	bell	21	taxi stand
3	mirror	22	taxi(cab)/cab
4	cable	23	meter
5	headlight	24	fare
6	handlebars	25	(taxi) driver
7	seat	26	passenger
8	saddlebag	27	crash helmet
9	wheel	28	goggles
10	mudguard	29	motor scooter
11	tire	30	rear light
12	spokes	31	seat
13	valve	32	accelerator
14	brake	33	brake
15	crossbar	34	saddlebag
16	pump	35	exhaust
17	pedal	36	starter
18	chain	37	footrest
19	sprocket	38	gearshift

1	train	16	gateman
2	engineer	17	gate
3	engine	18	waiting room
4	coach	19	passengers
5	compartment	20	platform
6	conductor	21	platform number
7	ticket	22	signalman
8	seat	23	signal box
9	luggage rack	24	(railroad) track
10	brakeman	25	(railroad) ties
11	flag	26	(railroad) switch
12	whistle	27	signals
13	(train) station	28	freight car
14	ticket office	29	buffer
15	schedule	30	siding

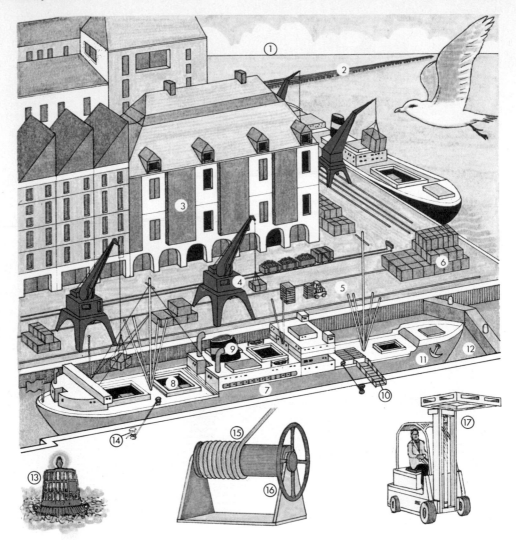

1 horizon	10 gangway
2 pier	11 anchor
3 warehouse	12 dock
4 crane	13 buoy
5 wharf	14 bollard
6 cargo	15 cable
7 ship	16 windlass
8 hold	17 forklift
9 smokestack	

1	sailboat	12	outboard motor
2	sail	13	bow
3	mast	14	stern
4	rudder	15	ferry
5	keel	16	barge
6	rowboat	17	trawler
7	oar	18	tanker
8	oarlock	19	deck
9	canoe	20	ocean liner
10	paddle	21	smokestack
11	motorboat		

1 customs	12 jet engine
2 customs officer	13 tail/tail fin
3 passport	14 glider
4 luggage/baggage	15 helicopter
5 captain/pilot	16 rotor
6 passenger	17 light aircraft
7 stewardess/flight attendant	18 propeller
8 steward/flight attendant	19 runway
9 (air)plane/airliner	20 control tower
10 fuselage	21 hangar
11 wing	

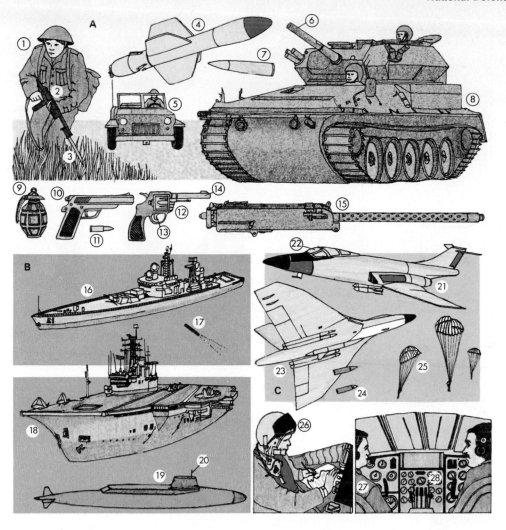

A. **Army**
1   soldier
2   rifle
3   bayonet
4   guided missile
5   jeep
6   gun
7   shell
8   tank
9   (hand) grenade
10 pistol
11 bullet/cartridge
12 revolver
13 trigger
14 barrel
15 machine gun

B. **Navy**
16 warship
17 torpedo
18 aircraft carrier
19 submarine
20 periscope

C. **Air Force**
21 fighter plane
22 cockpit
23 bomber
24 bomb
25 parachute
26 navigator
27 pilot
28 control panel

A. (Horse) Racing	**C. Basketball**
1 jockey	15 basket
2 (race)horse	16 backboard
3 saddle	17 ball
4 reins	
5 bridle	**D. Field Hockey**
6 bit	18 stick
7 stirrup	
8 jodhpurs	**E. Ping-Pong/Table-Tennis**
9 cap	19 racket
	20 net
	21 table
B. Boxing	
10 referee	**F. Wrestling**
11 boxer	22 wrestlers
12 (boxing) glove	
13 ring	**G. Judo**
14 ropes	23 judo suit

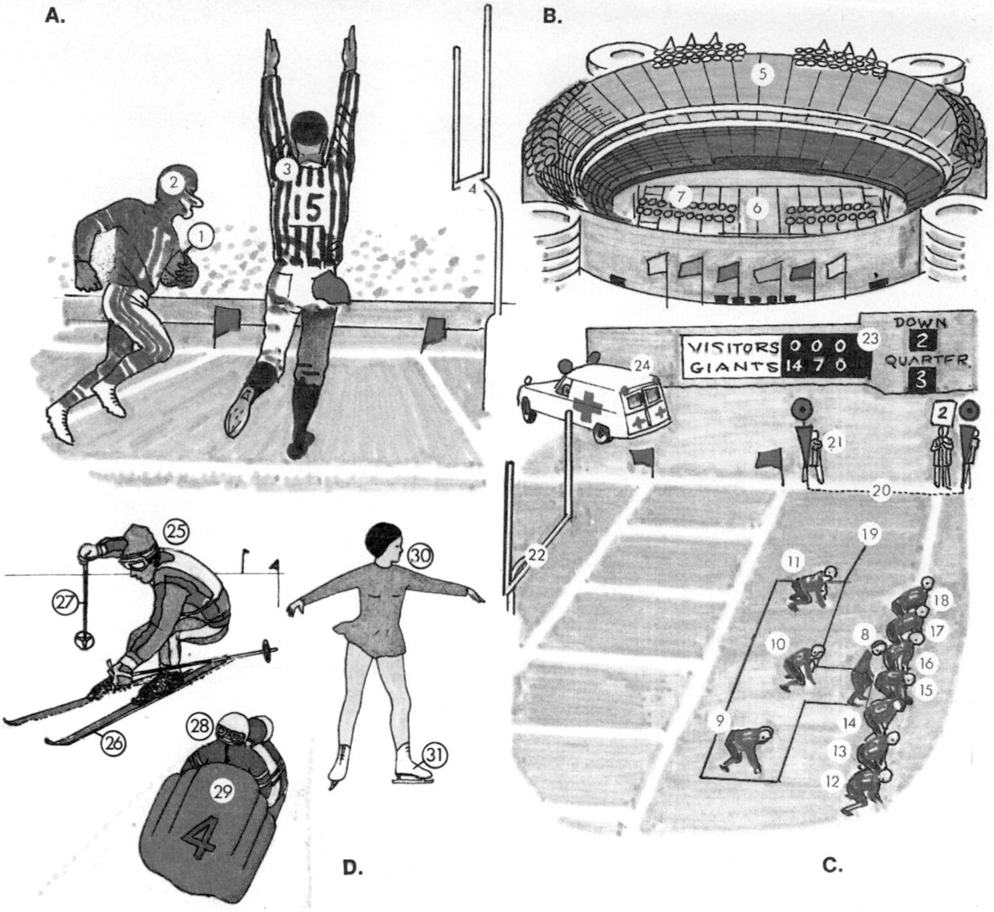

A. Football
1 football
2 helmet
3 referee
4 goalpost

B. Stadium
5 (grand)stand
6 field
7 lights

C. Line-Up
8 quarterback
9 right halfback
10 fullback
11 left halfback
12 right end
13 right tackle
14 right guard
15 center
16 left guard
17 left tackle
18 left end
19 T formation
20 chain
21 linesman
22 goalpost
23 scoreboard
24 ambulance

D. Winter Sports
25 skier
26 ski
27 (ski) pole
28 tobogganist
29 toboggan
30 (ice)skater
31 (ice)skate

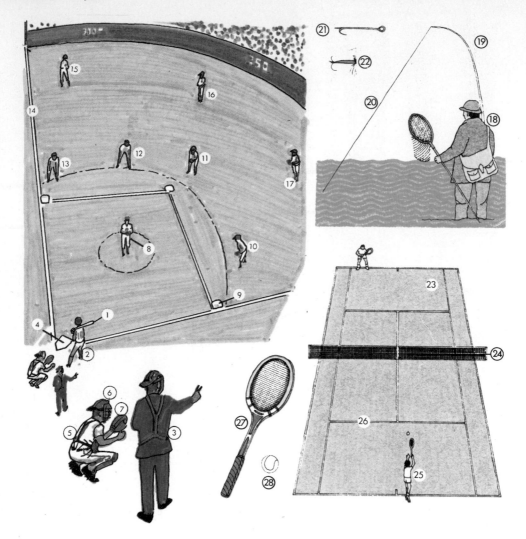

Baseball
1   bat
2   batter
3   umpire
4   home plate
5   catcher
6   catcher's mask
7   mitt/glove
8   pitcher
9   first base
10   first baseman
11   second baseman
12   shortstop
13   third baseman
14   foul line
15   left fielder
16   center fielder
17   right fielder

Fishing
18   fisherman
19   (fishing) rod
20   line
21   hook
22   bait

Tennis
23   (tennis) court
24   net
25   server
26   service line
27   (tennis) racket
28   (tennis) ball

Orchestra

1   clarinet
2   valve
3   musician/player
4   violin
5   strings
6   bow
7   viola
8   cello
9   double bass
10   conductor
11   baton
12   (sheet) music
13   rostrum
14   horn
15   piano
16   keys

17   pedal
18   stool
19   trumpet
20   trombone
21   slide
22   saxophone
23   mouthpiece

Pop Group

24   singer
25   microphone
26   (electric) guitar
27   amplifier
28   (loud)speaker
29   cymbals
30   drum

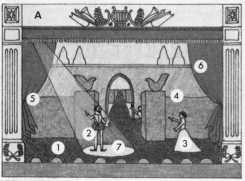
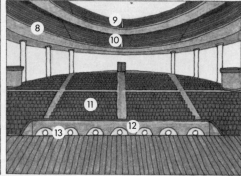
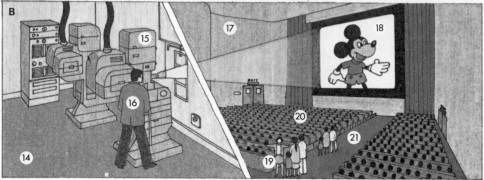

A. The Theater	**B. The Movies**
1 stage	14 projection room
2 actor	15 projector
3 actress	16 projectionist
4 set	17 movie theater
5 wings	18 screen
6 curtain	19 usherette
7 spotlight	20 seats
8 theater	21 aisle
9 gallery	
10 balcony	**C. The Library**
11 orchestra	22 librarian
12 (orchestra) pit	23 card catalog
13 footlights	24 desk
	25 bookshelf

1 (beer) bottle	18 cocktail waitress
2 bottle top	19 bartender
3 stein/mug	20 tap
4 (beer) can	21 (bar)stool
5 matchbook	22 waiter
6 match	23 customer
7 bottle opener	24 menu
8 cigarette	25 bottle of wine
9 ash	26 cork
10 ashtray	27 (wine) glass
11 corkscrew	28 saltshaker
12 straw	29 pepper mill
13 soft drink	30 pepper shaker
14 lighter	31 tablecloth
15 bar	32 napkin
16 draft beer	33 check
17 hard liquor	34 jigger

A.   Chess and Checkers
1   chess set
2   board
3   pawn
4   castle/rook
5   knight
6   bishop
7   queen
8   king
9   checkers

B.   Cards
10   (deck of) cards
11   jack of clubs
12   queen of diamonds
13   king of hearts
14   ace of spades

C.   Reading
15   book
16   cover
17   (dust) jacket
18   spine
19   page
20   illustration
21   text

D.   Photography
22   photograph/photo
23   negative
24   (roll of) film
25   camera
26   lens
27   screen
28   stand
29   (slide) projector
30   slide

1	sewing machine	14	ruffle
2	tape	15	button
3	seam	16	buttonhole
4	hem	17	stitch
5	thimble	18	knitting needle
6	needle	19	wool
7	elastic	20	pattern
8	(spool of) thread	21	knitting
9	lace	22	zipper
10	safety pin	23	hook and eye
11	pleat	24	ribbon
12	(common)/(straight) pin	25	tape measure
13	material/cloth	26	scissors
		27	snap

1 hairdresser	9 typist
2 butcher	10 dressmaker
3 carpenter	11 waitress
4 bank teller	12 truck driver
5 mechanic	13 clown
6 longshoreman	14 redcap/porter
7 miner	15 announcer
8 artist	

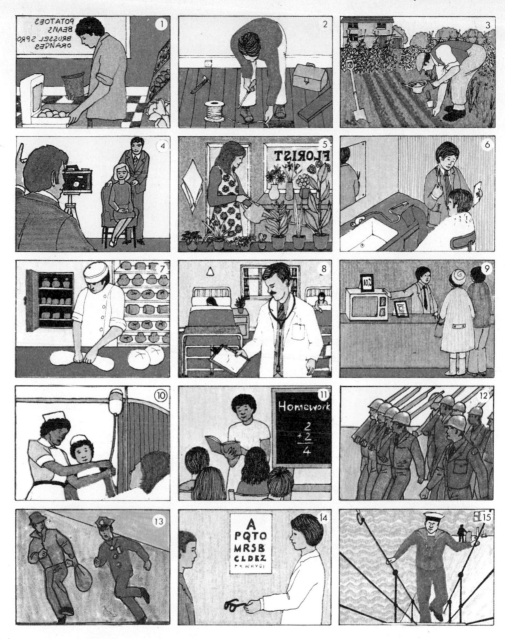

1 fruit seller	9 salesman
2 electrician	10 nurse
3 gardener	11 teacher
4 photographer	12 soldier
5 florist	13 policeman
6 barber	14 optician
7 baker	15 sailor
8 doctor	

1 horse	14 puppy
2 foal	15 cat
3 pig	16 kitten
4 snout	17 paw
5 llama	18 mouse
6 camel	19 squirrel
7 hump	20 rabbit
8 buffalo	21 whisker
9 horn	22 rat
10 donkey	23 tail
11 reindeer	24 fox
12 antler	25 bat
13 dog	26 hedgehog

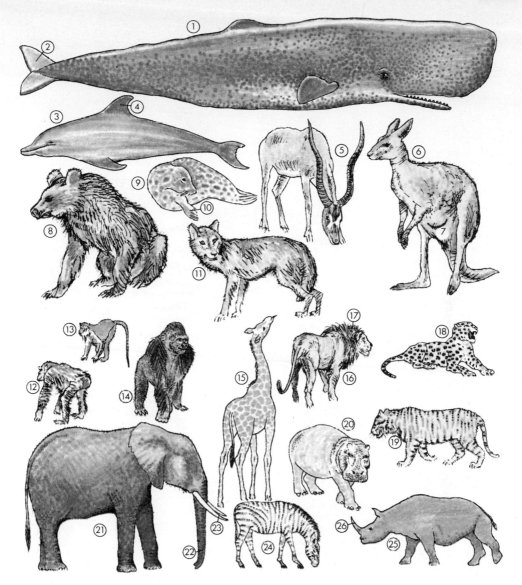

1 whale	14 gorilla
2 tail/fluke	15 giraffe
3 dolphin	16 lion
4 fin	17 mane
5 antelope	18 leopard
6 kangaroo	19 tiger
7 pouch	20 hippopotamus
8 bear	21 elephant
9 seal	22 trunk
10 flipper	23 tusk
11 wolf	24 zebra
12 baboon	25 rhinoceros
13 monkey	26 horn

Fish and Other Animals

1 shark	14 shell
2 fin	15 sunfish
3 swordfish	16 oyster
4 salmon	17 crab
5 gill	18 pincer/claw
6 herring	19 slug
7 tail	20 frog
8 snout	21 worm
9 scales	22 centipede
10 eel	23 octopus
11 jellyfish	24 tentacle
12 lobster	25 spider
13 snail	26 (spider) web
	27 scorpion

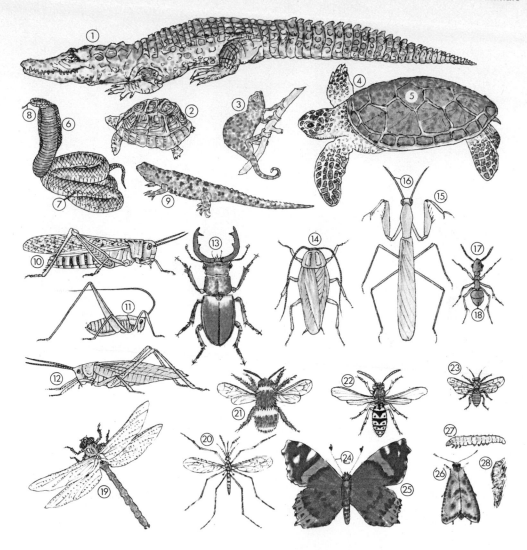

Reptiles
1 crocodile
2 tortoise
3 chameleon
4 turtle
5 shell
6 snake
7 scale
8 tongue
9 lizard

Insects
10 locust
11 cricket
12 grasshopper
13 beetle
14 cockroach
15 mantis
16 feeler
17 ant
18 abdomen
19 dragonfly
20 mosquito
21 bee
22 wasp
23 fly
24 antenna
25 butterfly
26 moth
27 caterpillar
28 cocoon

Birds

1	ostrich	17	swan
2	eagle	18	canary
3	claw	19	bill
4	beak	20	parrot
5	feathers	21	(sea)gull
6	hawk	22	swallow
7	owl	23	wing
8	flamingo	24	dove
9	webbed foot	25	goose
10	vulture	26	parakeet
11	peacock	27	hummingbird
12	crest	28	sparrow
13	penguin	29	nest
14	pheasant	30	kingfisher
15	heron	31	pigeon
16	turkey	32	blackbird
		33	crow

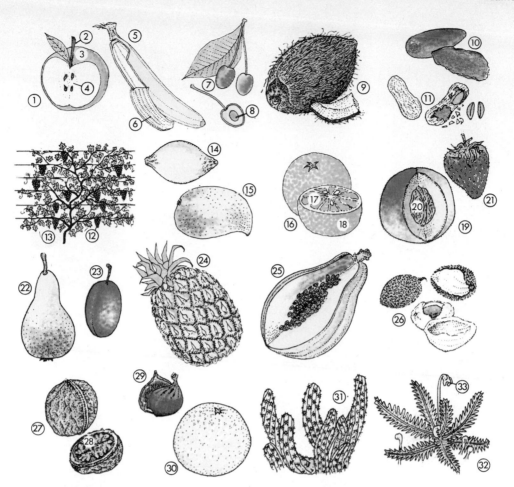

Fruit

1 apple	17 sections
2 stalk	18 peel/rind
3 skin	19 peach
4 core	20 pit/pip/stone
5 banana	21 strawberry
6 peel	22 pear
7 cherry	23 plum
8 pit/stone	24 pineapple
9 coconut	25 papaya
10 date	26 litchi
11 peanut	27 walnut
12 grapes	28 nutmeat
13 vine	29 fig
14 lemon	30 grapefruit
15 mango	31 cactus
16 orange	32 fern
	33 frond

Vegetables
1 bean
2 stalk
3 pea
4 pod
5 carrot
6 potato
7 squash
8 cucumber
9 beet
10 cauliflower
11 cabbage
12 lettuce
13 onion
14 mushroom
15 tomato
16 eggplant

Flowers
17 daffodil
18 daisy
19 rose
20 petal
21 orchid
22 tulip
23 stem
24 hibiscus
25 bud
26 waterlily
27 sunflower
28 seeds

1	(ear of) corn	13	branch/bough
2	wheat	14	twig
3	olive	15	leaf
4	cocoa bean	16	acorn
5	coffee berry	17	bark
6	cotton	18	log
7	rice	19	palm
8	tea	20	fir
9	sugar cane	21	(pine)cone
10	oak tree	22	(pine) needles
11	roots	23	cedar
12	trunk	24	willow

1 blow	14 dream
2 break	15 drive
3 carry	16 drown
4 catch	17 eat
5 climb	18 fall
6 crawl	19 fight
7 cry/weep	20 fly
8 cut	21 jump/leap
9 dance	22 kick
10 dig	23 kneel
11 dive	24 laugh
12 draw	25 lick
13 drink	

1 listen	14 sing
2 open	15 sit
3 lie	16 smile
4 paint	17 stand
5 pull	18 stir
6 push	19 sweep
7 read	20 swim
8 ride	21 tear
9 run	22 touch
10 sail	23 tie
11 sew	24 walk
12 shoot	25 wash
13 shut	

1 wave	13 pass
2 write	14 frown
3 wind	15 put
4 bend	16 spin
5 hit/beat	17 clap
6 hug	18 iron
7 kiss	19 sleep
8 pick	20 hold
9 throw	21 type
10 turn	22 boil
11 give	23 chop
12 comb	

1	carton	
2	paper bag/sack	
3	plastic garden bag	
4	sandwich bag	
5	bottle	
6	jar	
7	can	
8	paper cup	
9	thermos	
10	plastic wrap	
11	aluminum foil	

12	trash can	
13	barrel	
14	basket	
15	box	
16	trunk	
17	crate	
18	shopping bag	
19	suitcase	
20	carry-on case	
21	wallet	

A.   Lines
1   spiral
2   straight line
3   curve
4   perpendicular line
5   parallel lines
6   zigzag
7   wavy line

B.   Triangles
8   apex
9   base
10 obtuse angle
11 acute angle
12 hypotenuse

C.   Square
13 side
14 right angle

D.   Rectangle/Oblong
15 diagonal

E.   Circle
16 arc
17 radius
18 circumference
19 diameter
20 center
21 section

F.   Oval/Ellipse

G.   Solid Figures
22 pyramid
23 cone
24 cube
25 cylinder

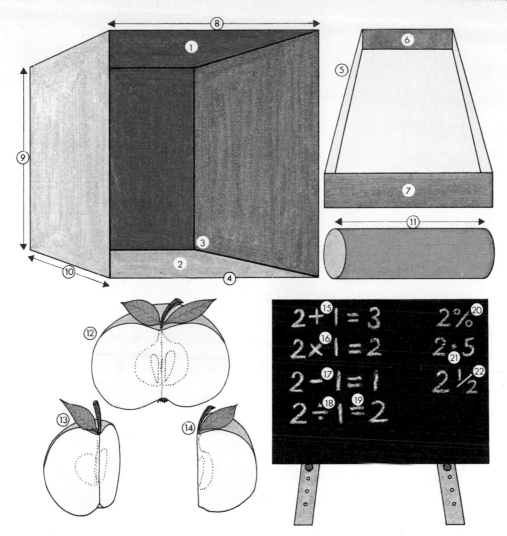

On the blackboard:

$$2 + 1 = 3 \qquad 2\%$$
$$2 \times 1 = 2 \qquad 2.5$$
$$2 - 1 = 1 \qquad 2\tfrac{1}{2}$$
$$2 \div 1 = 2$$

1	top	12	a half
2	bottom	13	a third
3	corner	14	a quarter
4	edge	15	plus
5	side	16	multiplied by
6	back	17	minus
7	front	18	divided by
8	width	19	equals
9	height	20	per cent
10	depth	21	decimal point
11	length	22	fraction

The Time

1 minute hand
2 hour hand
3 second hand
4 clock face
5 9:00: nine o'clock
6 9:10: ten after nine/nine-ten
7 9:15: a quarter after nine/nine-fifteen
8 9:30: nine-thirty
9 9:45: a quarter of ten/nine forty-five
10 9:50: ten of ten/nine-fifty

The Date

11 calendar
Today's date is Wednesday the sixteenth
of July/July sixteenth nineteen eighty:
July 16, 1980 or 7/16/80.

The Temperature

12 thermometer
The temperature is 18 degrees Centigrade (18°C)
or 65 degrees Fahrenheit (65°F).

1 Alan and Ann are **husband** and **wife.**
2 Their **children** are Betty and Bob.
3 Their **daughter** is Betty and their **son** is Bob.
4 Alan is Bob's **father** and Ann is Bob's **mother.**
5 Betty is Bob's **sister** and Bob is Betty's **brother.**
6 Alan is Ben's **father-in-law** and Ann is his **mother-in-law.**
7 Ben is Alan and Ann's **son-in-law** and Brenda is their **daughter-in-law.**
8 Ben is Bob's **brother-in-law** and Brenda is Betty's **sister-in-law.**
9 Colin is Cliff and Carol's **cousin.**
10 Betty is Colin's **aunt** and Ben is his **uncle.**
11 Colin is Betty's **nephew** and Carol is Bob's **niece.**
12 Cliff is Ann and Alan's **grandson** and Carol is their **granddaughter.**

1 bunch (of flowers)	9 pile (of stones)
2 bundle (of sticks)	10 herd (of cattle)
3 crowd (of people)	11 group (of tourists)
4 fleet (of ships)	12 pile (of blankets)
5 flight (of stairs)	13 plate (of sandwiches)
6 flock (of sheep or birds)	14 row (of houses)
7 gang (of workmen)	15 team (of players)
8 string (of beads)	16 swarm (of bees)

1 ball (of string/twine)	8 piece (of cake)
2 box (of cookies)	9 spool (of thread)
3 bar (of soap)	10 box (of matches)
4 glass (of milk)	pack (of cigarettes)
5 bottle (of wine)	11 cup (of coffee)
6 loaf (of bread)	12 roll (of paper)
7 lump (of sugar)	13 tube (of toothpaste)
	14 bowl (of soup)

1	a) big/large	9	a) fast
	b) little/small		b) slow
2	a) blunt	10	a) fat
	b) sharp		b) thin
3	a) clean	11	a) happy
	b) dirty		b) sad
4	a) closed/shut	12	a) easy
	b) open		b) difficult/hard
5	a) crooked	13	a) soft
	b) straight		b) hard
6	a) shallow	14	a) high
	b) deep		b) low
7	a) wet	15	a) hot
	b) dry		b) cold
8	a) empty	16	a) long
	b) full		b) short

1 a) narrow
   b) wide
2 a) young
   b) old
3 a) new
   b) old
4 a) calm
   b) rough
5 a) rough
   b) smooth
6 a) strong
   b) weak
7 a) neat
   b) sloppy/messy
8 a) good
   b) bad

9 a) pretty/beautiful
   b) ugly
10 a) first
   b) last
11 a) llght
   b) dark
12 a) light
   b) heavy
13 a) loud
   b) soft
14 a) solid
   b) hollow
15 a) thick
   b) thin
16 a) loose
   b) tight

1	**outside** the room	10	**in/inside** the drawer
2	**through** the door	11	**out of** the drawer
3	**below** the picture	12	**on** the table
4	**down** the wall	13	**on to/onto** the table
5	**up** the wall	14	**beside/next to** the table
6	**around** the neck	15	**by/near** the chair
7	**in front of** the chair	16	**behind** the chair
8	**against** the wall	17	**under/underneath/beneath** the table
9	**into** the drawer		

1	**above** the trees	7	**across/on** the road
2	**beyond** the bridge	8	**at** the corner
3	**from** the beach	9	**along** the road
4	**to** the beach	10	**toward** the bridge
5	**among** the trees	11	**away from** the bridge
6	**off** the road	12	**between** the cars

There is both an English Index and a French Index in this text. The French Index lists each word used in the dictionary with its page and item number. The English Index includes a pronunciation guide and a phonemic transcription for each English word in the book.

There are two numbers after each word in each index.

The first number refers to the page where the word is listed. The second number refers to the item number of the word.

For example: **abdomen** /ǽbdəmən/**59**/18 means that the word "abdomen" is the eighteenth item on page 59.

Vowels

/a/ as in calm /kam/	/ə/ as in butter /bə́tər/	/ɔ/ as in cough /kɔf/
/æ/ as in hat /hæt/	/i/ as in leak /lik/	/u/ as in broom /brum/
/e/ as in wait /wet/	/ɪ/ as in lick /lɪk/	/ʊ/ as in book /bʊk/
/ɛ/ as in wet /wɛt/	/o/ as in note /not/	

Consonants

/b/ as in base /bes/	/k/ as in cat /kæt/	/š/ as in ship /šɪp/
/č/ as in chip /čɪp/	/l/ as in lick /lɪk/	/t/ as in tin /tɪn/
/d/ as in dog /dɔg/	/m/ as in man /mæn/	/θ/ as in thin /θɪn/
/ð/ as in this /ðɪs/	/n/ as in win /wɪn/	/v/ as in vase /ves/
/f/ as in five /faɪv/	/ŋ/ as in sing /sɪŋ/	/w/ as in waist /west/
/g/ as in girl /gərl/	/p/ as in pin /pɪn/	/y/ as in yard / yard/
/h/ as in hand /hænd/	/r/ as in red /rɛd/	/z/ as in zebra /zíbrə/
/ǰ/ as in jacket /ǰǽkɪt/	/s/ as in sip /sɪp/	/ž/ as in measure /mɛ́žər/

/´/ over a vowel shows that the vowel has strong stress, eg. *address* /ǽdrɛs/ (noun), /ədrɛ́s/ (verb); *present* /prɛ́zɪnt/ (noun), /prɪzɛ́nt/ (verb).

INDEX

camera /kǽmrə/**52**/25
camping /kǽmpɪŋ/**35**
campstove /kǽmp-stov/**35**/5
camping stove /kǽmpɪŋ-stov/**35**/5
can /kæn/**30**/22; **51**/4; **67**/7
canary /kənǽri/**60**/18
canned food /kǽnd-fúd/**20**/16
canoe /kənú/**43**/9
can-opener /kǽn-opənər/**30**/21
cap /kæp/**46**/9
capsule /kǽpsəl/**4**/19
captain /kǽptən/**44**/5
car /kar/**15**/30; **38**; **39**/16
car radio /kár-redio/**38**/25
carbon paper /kárbən-pepər/**21**/20
card /kard/**52**/10
card catalog /kárd-kætələg/**50**/23
card file /kárd-faɪl/**21**/26
cardigan /kárdɪgən/**10**/9
cargo /kárgo/**42**/6
Caribbean Sea /kærɪbíən-si/**6**/18
carpenter /kárpɪntər/**54**/3
carpet /kárpɪt/**29**/3
carrot /kǽrət/**62**/5
carry /kǽri/**64**/3
carry on case /kǽri-an-kes/**67**/20
carton /kártən/**67**/1
cartridge /kártrɪj/**45**/11
cashier /kæšír/**20**/2
cash register /kǽš-rɛjɪstər/**20**/3
Caspian Sea /kǽspiən-sí/**6**/24
castle /kǽsəl/**52**/4
cat /kæt/**56**/15
catch /kæč/**64**/4
catcher /kǽčər/**48**/5
catcher's mask /kǽčərz-mæsk/**48**/6
caterpillar /kǽtərpɪlər/**59**/27
cauliflower /káliflauər/**62**/10
cedar /sídər/**63**/23
ceiling /sílɪŋ/**29**/1
cell /sɛl/**16**/15
cello /čɛlo/**49**/8
cement /sɪmɛ́nt/**23**/16
cement mixer /sɪmɛ́nt-mɪksər/**23**/21
centigrade /sɛ́ntɪgred/**70**/12
centipede /sɛ́ntɪpid/**58**/22
center /sɛ́ntər/**47**/15; **68**/20
center fielder /sɛ́ntər fíldər/**48**/16
chain /čen/**40**/18; **47**/20
chair /čɛr/**29**/13; **30**/27
chalk /čɔk/**18**/4
chameleon /kəmílíən/**59**/3
changing table /čɛ́njɪŋ-tebəl/**32**/32
check /čɛk/**51**/33
checkers /čɛkərz/**52**; **52**/9
checkout counter /čɛ́kaut-kauntər/**20**/4
cheek /čik/**9**/5
cheese /čiz/**20**/9
cherry /čɛ́ri/**61**/7
chess /čɛs/**52**
chess set /čɛ́s-sɛt/**52**/1
chest /čɛst/**8**/14
chest of drawers /čɛ́st-ə-drɔərz/**32**/16
chick /čɪk/**36**/35
chicken /číkɪn/**36**/33
children /číldrɪn/**71**/2
chimney /čímni/**26**/2
chin /čɪn/**9**/6
chisel /čízəl/**24**/4
choke /čok/**38**/15
chop /čap/**66**/23
cigarette /sígərɛt/**51**/8
circle /sárkəl/**39**/4; **68**
circumference /sərkʌ́mfrəns/**68**/18
city /síti/**14-15**
clap /klæp/**66**/17
clarinet /klærɪnɛ́t/**49**/1
claw /klɔ/**58**/18
clean /klin/**74**/3a
clerk /klərk/**20**/8
cliff /klɪf/**35**/6
climb /kláim/**64**/5
clip /klɪp/**12**/23
clock-face /klák-fes/**70**/4
closed /klozd/**74**/4a
closet /klázət/**32**/14
cloth /klɔθ/**53**/13
clothes /kloz/**10-13**
clothesline /klóz-laɪn/**27**/28

clothespin /klóz-pɪn/**27**/30
cloud /kláud/**27**/2
clown /kláun/**54**/13
clutch /kləč/**38**/20
coach /koč/**41**/4
coastline /kóst-laɪn/**5**/11
coal /kol/**37**/9
coat /kot/**11**/14; **13**/11
coatrack /kót-ræk/**28**/9
cockpit /kákpɪt/**45**/22
cockroach /kákroč/**59**/14
cocktail waitress /káktel-wetrɪs/**51**/18
cocoa bean /kóko-bin/**63**/4
coconut /kókənət/**61**/9
cocoon /kəkún/**59**/28
coffee berry /kɔ́fi-bɛri/**63**/5
coffee pot /kɔ́fi-pat/**30**
coffee table /kɔ́fi-tebəl/**29**/23
coin /kɔ́ɪn/**20**/25
cold /kold/**74**/15b
cold water faucet /kold-wɔtər-fɔsɪt/**33**/3
collar /kálər/**11**/2
collar bone /kálər-bon/**8**/2
comb /kom/**12**/19; **32**/22; **66**/12
combine (noun) /kámbaɪn/**36**/16
comet /kámət/**4**/1
common pin /kámən-pín/**53**/12
compact /kámpækt/**12**/12
compartment /kəmpártmɪnt/**41**/5
compass /kámpəs/**5**; **18**/11
conductor /kəndáktər/**41**/6; **49**/10
cone /kon/**63**/21; **68**/23
Congo /kángo/**7**/50
constellation /kánstəlésən/**4**/2
container /kənténər/**67**
continent /kántɪnənt/**6**
control panel /kəntról-pænəl/**45**/28
control tower /kəntról-tauər/**44**/20
convertible /kənvártəbəl/**38**/38
cookie /kúki/**20**/20
cooling tower /kúlɪŋ-tauər/**37**/8
Coral Sea /kórəl-sí/**6**/29
cord /kərd/**28**/21; **31**/12
core /kor/**61**/4
cork /kɔrk/**51**/26
corkscrew /kɔ́rk-skru/**51**/11
corn /kɔrn/**63**/1
corner /kɔ́rnər/**69**/3
cottage /kátɪj/**35**/8
cotton /kátən/**63**/6
couch /kauč/**29**/9
counter /káuntər/**22**/3; **30**/8
country /kántri/**34**
court /kort/**48**/23
court of law /kɔrt-əv-lɔ́/**16c**
cousin /kázɪn/**71**/9
cover /kóvər/**52**/16
cow /kau/**36**/21
cowshed /káu-šed/**36**/3
crab /kræb/**58**/17
crackers /krǽkərz/**20**/26
crane /kren/**23**/1; **42**/4
crashhelmet /krǽš-hɛlmɪt/**40**/27
crate /kret/**67**/17
crawl /krɔl/**64**/6
crescent moon /krɛ́sənt-mún/**4**/11
crest /krɛst/**60**/12
crib /krɪb/**32**/26
cricket /kríkɪt/**59**/15
crocodile /krákədaɪl/**59**/1
crooked /krúkɪd/**74**/5a
crossbar /krɔ́s-bar/**40**/15
crosswalk /krɔ́s-wɔk/**14**/2
crow /kro/**60**/33
crowd /kráud/**72**/3
crowd of people /kráud-əv-pipəl/**72**r
crutch /kráč/**17**/26
cry /kráɪ/**64**/7
crystal /krístəl/**19**/17
cube /kyub/**68**/24
cucumber /kyúkəmbər/**62**/8
cuff /kəf/**11**/3; **18**
cuff links /kəf-lɪŋks/**11**/25
cup /kəp/**30**/37; **73**/11
cup of coffee /kəp-əv-kɔfi/**73**/11
curb /kərb/**14**/8
curtain /kártən/**26**/14; **29**/7; **50**/6
curtain rod /kártən-rad/**33**/30
curve /kərv/**68**/3

cushion /kúšən/**29**/10
customer /kástəmər/**20**/5; **51**/23
customs /kástəmz/**44**/1
customs officer /kástəmz-ɔfɪsər/**44**/2
cut /kət/**64**/8
cylinder /sílɪndər/**68**/25
cylinder head /sílɪndər-hɛd/**38**/36
cymbal /símbəl/**49**/29

daffodil /dǽfədɪl/**62**/17
daisy /dézi/**62**/18
dam /dæm/**37**/2
dance /dæns/**64**/9
Danube /dǽnyub/**7**/47
dark /dark/**75**/11b
dashboard /dáš-bord/**38**/12
date /det/**61**/10; **70**
daughter /dɔ́tər/**71**/3
daughter-in-law /dɔ́tər-ɪn-lɔ/**71**/7
decimal point /dɛ́sɪməl-pɔ́ɪnt/**69**/21
deck /dɛk/**43**/19
deck chair /dɛ́k-čɛr/**35**/19
deck of cards /dɛ́k-əv-kárdz/**52**/10
deep /dip/**74**/6b
defense /difɛ́ns/**45**
defendant /difɛ́ndənt/**16**/20
defense attorney /difɛ́ns-ətórni/**16**/21
degree /dɪgrí/**70**/12
delta /dɛ́ltə/**5**/9
dental assistant /dɛ́ntəl-əsɪstənt/**17**/14
dentist /dɛ́ntɪst/**17**; **17**/16
dentist's chair /dɛ́ntɪsts-čɛr/**17**/15
depth /dɛpθ/**69**/10
derrick /dɛ́rɪk/**37**/10
deserts /dɛ́zərts/**7**
desk /dɛsk/**18**/7; **21**/1; **32**/15; **50**/24
detection /ditɛ́kšən/**16**
diagonal /daɪǽgənəl/**68**/15
dial /daɪl/**19**/5; **28**/20
diameter /daɪǽmətər/**68**/19
diaper /dáɪpər/**32**/36
difficult /dífɪkəlt/**74**/12b
dig /dɪg/**64**/10
dirty /dárti/**74**/3b
dish towel /díš-tauəl/**30**/25
dish washer /díš-wɔšər/**30**/24
display window /dɪsplé-windo/**15**/21
distributor /dɪstríbyutər/**38**/34
dive /daɪv/**64**/11
diverter /dɪvártər/**33**/7
divide by /dɪváɪd baɪ/**69**/18
dock /dak/**42**/12
doctor /dáktər/**17**/21; **55**/8
dog /dɔg/**56**/13
doll /dal/**32**/31
dolphin /dálfɪn/**57**/3
donkey /dɔ́ŋki/**56**/10
door /dɔr/**26**/7; **28**/1
doormat /dɔ́r-mæt/**26**/18; **28**/6
double bass /dábəl-bes/**49**/9
dove /dəv/**60**/24
down /dáun/**76**/4
downstairs /dáunstérz/**28**/15
dragonfly /drǽgən-flaɪ/**59**/19
drain /dren/**14**/10; **33**/5
drainpipe /drén-paɪp/**23**/9; **26**/17
drain plug /drén-pləg/**33**/6
draft beer /drǽft-bír/**51**/14
drape /drep/**29**/8
draw /drɔ/**64**/12
dream /drim/**64**/14
dress /drɛs/**13**/10
dressing table /drɛ́sɪŋ-tebəl/**32**/10
dressing table skirt /drɛ́sɪŋ-tebəl skərt/**32**/11
dressmaker /drɛ́s-mekər/**54**/10
drill /drɪl/**17**/17
drink /drɪŋk/**64**/13
drive /dráɪv/**64**/15
driver /dráɪvər/**40**/25
drown /dráun/**64**/16
drum /drám/**49**/30
duck /dək/**36**/32
duckling /dáklɪŋ/**36**/31
dump truck /dámp-trək/**23**/22
dust brush /dást-brəš/**31**/6
dustcloth /dástklɔθ/**31**/7
dust jacket /dást-jækɪt/**52**/17
dust pan /dást-pæn/**31**/8

eagle /ígəl/**60**/2
ear /ɪr/**9**/3
ear of corn /ír-əv-kórn/**63**/1
earring /ír-rɪŋ/**12**/9
Earth /ɔ́rθ/**4**/7
east /ist/**5**/16
East China Sea /íst-čáɪnə-sí/**7**/32
easy /ízi/**74**/12a
eat /it/**64**/17
eclipse /ɪklíps/**4**/10
edge /ɛǰ/**69**/4
education /ɛjukéšən/**18–19**
eel /il/**58**/10
egg /ɛg/**20**/11
eggplant /ég-plænt/**62**/16
elastic /ɪlǽstɪk/**53**/7
elbow /élbo/**8**/23
electric can opener /ɪléktrɪk-kǽn-opənər/**30**/19
electric drill /ɪléktrɪk-dríl/**25**/4
electric guitar /ɪléktrɪk-gɪtár/**49**/26
electrician /ɪlɛktríšən/**55**/2
elephant /éləfənt/**57**/21
ellipse /ɪlíps/**68**
emergency brake /ɪmɔ́rǰɪnsi-brek/**38**/19
empty /émpti/**74**/8a
end table /énd-tebəl/**29**/25
engine /énjɪn/**38**/31; **41**/3
engineer /enjɪnír/**41**/2
envelope /énvəlop/**21**/11; **22**/10, 15
equal /íkwəl/**69**/19
Equator /ikwétər/**5**/4
eraser /irésər/**18**/3
estuary /éstyuɛri/**5**/10
Europe /yárəp/**6**/3
excavator /ékskəvetər/**23**/20
exhaust /ɪgzɔ́st/**38**/7; **40**/35
expressway /ɪksprés-we/**39**/1
extension cord /ɪksténšən-kɔrd/**24**/10
eye /áɪ/**9**/1
eyeball /áɪ-bɔl/**9**/15
eyebrow /áɪ-brau/**9**/16
eyelash /áɪ-læš/**9**/18
eyelid /áɪ-lɪd/**9**/17
eye shadow /áɪ-šædo/**12**/16

face /fes/**9**
face cream /fes-krim/**12**/17
Fahrenheit /fǽrɪnhaɪt/**70**/12
fall /fɔl/**64**/18
family /fǽmli/**71**
fare /fær/**40**/24
farm /farm/**36**
farmer /fármər/**36**/15
farm house /fárm-haus/**36**/7
fast /fæst/**74**/9a
fat /fæt/**74**/10a
father /fáðər/**71**/4
father-in-law /fáðər-ɪn-lɔ/**71**/6
feather /féðər/**60**/5
feeler /fílər/**59**/16
fence /fɛns/**36**/10
fern /fərn/**61**/32
ferry /féri/**43**/15
field /fild/**34**/13; **36**/8; **47**/6
field hockey /fíld-haki/**46**
fig /fɪg/**61**/29
fight /faɪt/**64**/19
fighter plane /fáɪtər-plen/**45**/21
figure /fígyər/**68**
file /faɪl/**21**/18; **24**/2
file cabinet /fáɪl-kæbɪnɪt/**21**/19
filing cabinet /fáɪlɪŋ-kæbɪnɪt/**21**/19
film /fɪlm/**52**/24
fin /fɪn/**57**/4; **58**/2
finger /fíŋgər/**8**/30
finger-nail /fíŋgər-nel/**8**/31
fingerprint /fíŋgər-prɪnt/**16**/11
fir /fər/**63**/20
fire /fáɪər/**17**; **17**/12; **29**/6
Fire Department /fáɪər-dɪpartmənt/**17**
fire engine /fáɪər-ɛnjɪn/**17**
fire escape /fáɪər-ɪskep/**17**/11
fire extinguisher /fáɪər-ɪkstɪŋgwɪšər/**17**/5
fire hose /fáɪər-hoz/**17**/3
fire hydrant /fáɪər-haɪdrənt/**17**/4
fireman /fáɪərmən/**17**/1
fireman's boot /fáɪərmənz-but/**17**/6
fireman's hat /fáɪərmənz hæt/**17**/2

fireplace /fáɪər-ples/**29**/4
fire truck /fáɪər-trək/**17**/7
first /fərst/**75**/10a
first base /fərst-bés/**48**/9
first baseman /fərst-bésmən/**48**/10
fish /fɪš/**20**/22; **58**
fisherman /fíšərmən/**48**/18
fishing /fíšɪŋ/**48**
fishing rod /fíšɪŋ-rad/**48**/19
fist /fɪst/**8**/26
flag /flæg/**41**/11
flamingo /fləmíngo/**60**/8
flap /flæp/**22**/16
flashlight /flǽš-laɪt/**16**/9
flask /flæsk/**19**/16
fleet /flit/**72**/4
fleet of ships /flit-əv-šips/**72**/4
flight /flaɪt/**72**/5
flight attendant /flaɪt-əténdənt/**44**/7, 8
flight of stairs /flaɪt-əv-stérz/**72**/5
flipper /flɪpər/**35**/21; **57**/10
flock /flak/**72**/6
flock of birds /flák-əv-bárdz/**72**/6
flock of sheep /flák-əv-šíp/**72**/6
floor /flɔr/**28**/7
florist /flɔ́rɪst/**55**/5
flower /fláuər/**27**/20; **62**
flower bed /fláuər-bed/**27**/21
flower pot /fláuər-pat/**27**/24
fluke /fluk/**57**/2
fly /flaɪ/**59**/23; **64**/20
foal /fol/**56**/2
folding rule /fóldɪŋ-rúl/**24**/12
foot /fut/**8**/37
football /fútbɔl/**47**; **47**/1
footlights /fút-laɪts/**50**/13
footpath /fút-pæθ/**34**/17
footprint /fút-prɪnt/**16**/12
footrest /fút-rest/**40**/37
forearm /fɔr-arm/**8**/24
forehead /fɔ́r-hɛd/**9**/8
forest /fɔ́rɪst/**34**/9
fork /fɔrk/**30**/33
forklift /fɔ́rk-lɪft/**42**/17
foul line /fául-laɪn/**48**/14
foundations /faundéšənz/**23**/10
fox /faks/**56**/24
fraction /frǽkšən/**69**/22
freeway /frí-we/**39**/1
freezer /frízər/**20**/14
freight car /frét-kar/**41**/28
frog /frɔg/**58**/20
from /frəm/**77**/3
frond /frand/**61**/33
front /frənt/**69**/7
front door /fránt-dór/**26**/7
frown /fraun/**66**/14
fruit /fruit/**20**/17; **30**/11; **61**
fruit basket /frút-bæskɪt/**30**/10
fruit seller /frút-sɛlər/**55**/1
fruit tree /frút-tri/**36**/11
frying pan /fráɪɪŋ-pæn/**30**/14
full /ful/**74**/8b
full moon /fúl-mun/**4**/13
full back /fúl-bæk/**47**/10
furrow /fáro/**36**/20
fuselage /fyúsəlaž/**44**/10

galaxy /gǽləksi/**4**/3
gallery /gǽləri/**50**/9
game /gem/**32**/20
gang /gæŋ/**72**/2
gang of workmen /gǽŋ-əv-wárkmɪn/**72**/7
Ganges /gǽnjiz/**7**/52
gangway /gǽŋwe/**42**/10
garage /gəráž/**26**/6
garbage can /gárbɪj-kæn/**30**/9
gardener /gárdnər/**55**/3
gas gauge /gǽs-gej/**38**/13
gas pump /gǽs-pəmp/**39**/8
gas station /gǽs-stešən/**39**/7
gas cap /gǽs-kæp/**38**/3
gate /get/**27**/16; **41**/17
gateman /gét-mæn/**41**/16
gearshift /gír-šɪft/**38**/21; **40**/38
gill /gɪl/**58**/5
giraffe /jərǽf/**57**/15
girl /gərl/**12–13**
give /gɪv/**66**/11

glass /glæs/**30**/36; **33**/18; **51**/27; **73**/4
glasses /glǽsɪz/**11**/23
glider /gláɪdər/**44**/14
globe /glob/**55**
glove /gləv/**11**/20; **48**/7
glue /glu/**18**/13
goalpost /gól-post/**47**/4,22
goat /got/**36**/24
Gobi /góbi/**7**/44
goggles /gágəlz/**35**/15; **40**/28
good /gud/**75**/8a
goose /gus/**60**/25
gorilla /gərílə/**57**/14
gown /gáun/**16**/24
granddaughter /grǽn-dɔtər/**71**/12
grandson /grǽn-sən/**71**/12
grandstand /grǽnd-stænd/**47**/5
grape /grep/**61**/12
grapefruit /grép-frut/**61**/30
grass /græs/**26**/21
grasshopper /grǽshapər/**59**/12
grenade /grənéd/**45**/9
grill /grɪl/**38**/27
groundcloth /gráund-klɔθ/**35**/2
group /grup/**72**/11
group of tourists /grúp-əv-tərɪsts/**72**/11
guard /gard/**16**/13
guided missile /gáɪdɪd-mísəl/**45**/4
guitar /gɪtár/**49**/26
gulf /gəlf/**6**
Gulf of Alaska /gólf-əv-əlǽskə/**6**/15
Gulf of Guinea /gólf-əv-gíni/**6**/19
Gulf of Mexico /gólf-əv-méksɪko/**6**/17
gull /gəl/**60**/21
gun /gən/**16**/2; **45**/6
gutter /gátər/**14**/9; **26**/16

hacksaw /hǽk-sɔ/**25**/18
hair /hær/**8**/9
hairbrush /hǽr-brəš/**32**/21
hairdresser /hǽr-drɛsər/**54**/1
hair dryer /hǽr-draɪər/**31**/14
half /hæf/**69**/12
half moon /hǽf-mún/**4**/12
hall /hɔl/**28**
hammer /hǽmər/**25**/14
hamper /hǽmpər/**33**/28
hand /hænd/**8**/27
hand brake /hǽnd-brek/**38**/19
handcuffs /hǽn-kəfs/**16**/8
hand drill /hǽn-drɪl/**25**/3
hand grenade /hǽn grəned/**45**/9
handkerchief /hǽŋkərčɪf/**13**/9
handle /hǽndəl/**25**/16
handlebars /hǽndəl-barz/**40**/6
hangar /hǽŋər/**44**/21
happy /hǽpi/**74**/11a
hard /hard/**74**/13b
hard liquor /hárd-líkər/**51**/17
hat /hæt/**11**/13
hatchet /hǽčɪt/**25**/7
hawk /hɔk/**60**/6
hay /he/**36**/2
hayloft /hé-lɔft/**36**/1
head /hɛd/**8**/10; **25**/15
headboard /héd-bɔrd/**32**/2
headlight /héd-laɪt/**38**/29; **40**/5
heart /hart/**9**/23
heavy /hévi/**75**/12b
hedge /hɛj/**27**/17; **34**/14
hedgehog /hɛj-hɔg/**56**/26
heel /hil/**9**/38; **11**/11
height /haɪt/**69**/9
helicopter /hélɪkaptər/**44**/15
helmet /hɛlmɪt/**47**/2
hem /hɛm/**53**/4
hen /hɛn/**36**/33
herd /hərd/**72**/10
herd of cattle /hərd-əv-kætəl/**72**/10
heron /hérən/**60**/15
herring /hérɪŋ/**58**/6
hibiscus /haɪbískəs/**62**/24
high /haɪ/**74**/14a
hill /hɪl/**34**/10
Himalayas /hɪməléəz/**7**/40
hinge /hɪnj/**28**/5
hip /hɪp/**8**/18
hip-bone /híp-bon/**8**/7
hippopotamus /hɪpəpátəməs/**57**/20

hit /hɪt/**66**/5
hobby /hábi/**52**
hod /had/**23**/18
hold /hold/**42**/8; **66**/20
hole puncher /hól-pənčər/**21**/6
hollow /hálo/**75**/14b
homeplate /hom-plét/**48**/4
hood /hʊd/**38**/26
hoof /hʊf/**36**/27
hook /hʊk/**28**/10; **48**/21
hook and eye /hʊk-ən-aí/**53**/23
horizon /həráɪzən/**42**/1
horn /hɔrn/**49**/14; **56**/9; **57**/26
horse /hɔrs/**36**/25; **46**/2; **56**/1
horse-racing /hɔ́rs-resɪŋ/**46**
hose /hoz/**17**/3
hospital bed /háspɪtəl-bed/**17**/19
hospital ward /haspɪtəl-wɔrd/**17**
hot /hat/**74**/15a
hot dog /hát-dɔg/**20**/12
hotel /hotél/**35**/7
hot water faucet /hát-wɔ́tər-fɔsɪt/**33**/2
hour hand /áʊər-hænd/**70**/2
house /háʊs/**26**
household /háʊs-hold/**31**
hubcap /hə́b-kæp/**38**/30
Hudson Bay /hə́dsən-bé/**6**/16
hug /həg/**66**/6
human /hyúmən/**8**
hummingbird /hə́mɪŋ-bərd/**60**/27
hump /həmp/**56**/7
husband /hə́zbənd/**71**/1
hydrant /háɪdrənt/**17**/4
hypoteneuse /haɪpátənus/**68**/12

icecream /áɪs-krím/**35**/17
ice skater /áɪs-sketər/**47**/30
ice skates /áɪs-skets/**47**/31
icicle /áɪsɪkəl/**27**/8
ignition /ɪgníšən/**38**/14
illustration /ɪləstréšən/**52**/20
in /ɪn/**76**/10
in box /ín-baks/**21**/12
Indian /índiən/**6**/13
Indus /índəs/**7**/51
in front of /ɪn-frónt-əv/**76**/7
insect /ínsɛkt/**59**
inside /ɪnsáɪd/**76**/10
inside lane /ínsaɪd-lén/**39**/6
insides /ɪnsáɪdz/**9**
instep /ínstɛp/**9**/39
intersection /íntərsɛkšən/**14**/15
intestines /ɪntéstɪnz/**9**/27
into /ɪn-tu/**76**/9
iris /áɪrɪs/**9**/20
iron /áɪərn/**31**/11; **66**/18
ironing board /áɪərnɪŋ-bɔrd/**31**/3
irrigation canal /ɪrɪgéšən-kənæl/**36**/17
island /áɪlənd/**5**/12

jack of clubs /jǽk-əv-klə́bz/**52**/11
jacket /jǽkɪt/**10**/7, 19; **11**/27;
   13/7; **29**/22; **52**/17
jail /jel/**16**
jar /jar/**67**/6
jaw /jɔ/**9**/9
jeans /jinz/**10**/14; **13**/14
jeep /jip/**45**/5
jellyfish /jéli-fiš/**58**/11
jet engine /jét-énjɪn/**44**/12
jewelry box /juəlri-baks/**32**/24
jigger /jígər/**51**/34
jockey /jáki/**46**/1
jodhpurs /jádpərz/**46**/8
judge /jəj/**16**/22
judo /júdo/**46**
judo suit /júdo sut/**46**/23
jump /jəmp/**64**/21
jury /jə́ri/**16**/17

Kalahari /kaləhári/**7**/42
kangaroo /kæŋgərú/**57**/6
keel /kil/**43**/5
kettle /kétəl/**30**/17
key /ki/**49**/16
kick /kɪk/**64**/22
kidney /kídni/**9**/26
king /kɪŋ/**52**/8

kingfisher /kíŋfɪšər/**60**/30
king of hearts /kíŋ-əv-hárts/**52**/13
kiss /kɪs/**66**/7
kitchen /kíčɪn/**30**
kite /káɪt/**35**/30
kitten /kítən/**56**/16
knee /ni/**8**/34
kneecap /ní-kæp/**8**/8
kneesock /ní-sak/**13**/12
kneel /nil/**64**/23
knife /náɪf/**30**/31
knight /náɪt/**52**/5
knitting /nítɪŋ/**53**/21
knitting needle /nítɪŋ-nidəl/**53**/18

lab /læb/**19**
label /lébəl/**22**/21
laboratory /lǽbrətori/**19**
lace /les/**53**/9
ladder /lǽdər/**17**/8; **23**/5
lake /lek/**5**/13; **34**/5
lamb /læm/**36**/30
lamp /læmp/**17**/18; **29**/26
lamp shade /lǽmp-šed/**29**/27
lapel /ləpél/**11**/15
large /larj/**74**/1a
last /læst/**75**/10b
laugh /læf/**64**/24
launch pad /lɔ́nč-pæd/**4**/17
launching pad /lɔ́nčɪŋ-pæd/**4**/17
laundry /lɔ́ndri/**27**/29
law /lɔ/**16**
lawn /lɔn/**27**/19
leaf /lif/**63**/15
leap /lip/**64**/21
leaves /livz/**27**/15
left end /left-énd/**47**/18
left fielder /léft-fíldər/**48**/15
left guard /left-gárd/**47**/16
left halfback /left-hǽlf-bæk/**47**/11
left lane /læft-lén/**39**/5
left tackle /læft-tǽkəl/**47**/17
leg /lɛg/**8**/32
leisure /lížər/**50**
lemon /lémən/**61**/14
length /lɛŋθ/**69**/11
lens /lɛnz/**19**/12; **52**/26
leopard /lépərd/**57**/18
lettuce /létəs/**62**/12
level /lévəl/**23**/19
librarian /laɪbrǽriən/**50**/22
library /láɪbræri/**50**
license plate /láɪsəns-plet/**38**/28
lick /lɪk/**64**/25
lie /láɪ/**65**/3
light /láɪt/**17**/18; **28**/16; **47**/7; **75**/11a, 12a
light aircraft /láɪt-ǽrkræft/**44**/17
light-bulb /láɪt-bəlb/**31**/13
lighter /láɪtər/**51**/14
lightning /láɪtnɪŋ/**27**/1
light-switch /láɪt-swɪč/**28**/17
line /láɪn/**48**/20; **68**;
line of latitude /láɪn-əv-lætitud/**5**/15
line of longitude /láɪn-əv-lɔnjitud/**5**/14
linesman /láɪnzmən/**47**/21
line-up /láɪn-əp/**47**
lion /láɪən/**57**/16
lip /lɪp/**9**/13
lipstick /lípstɪk/**12**/18
listen /lísən/**65**/1
litchi /líči/**61**/26
little/lítəl/**74**/16
liver /lívər/**9**/25
living-room /lívɪŋ-rum/**29**
lizard /lízərd/**59**/9
llama /lámə/**56**/5
loaf /lof/**73**/6
loafer /lófər/**10**/10
loaf of bread /lof-əv-bréd/**73**/6
lobster /lábstər/**58**/12
lock /lak/**28**/3
locust /lókəst/**59**/10
log /lɔg/**63**/18
long /lɔŋ/**74**/16a
longshoreman /lɔ́ŋ-šórmən/**54**/6
loose /lus/**75**/16a
loose-leaf notebook /lús-lif-not-bʊk/**18**/18
loose-leaf paper /lús-lif-pépər/**18**/17
loud /láʊd/**75**/13a

loudspeaker /láʊd-spikər/**49**/28
low/lo/**74**/14b
luggage /lə́gɪj/**44**/4
luggage rack /lə́gɪj-ræk/**41**/9
lump /ləmp/**73**/7
lump of sugar /ləmp-əv-šugər/**73**/7
lung /ləŋ/**9**/24

machine gun /məšín-gən/**45**/15
magazine /mægəzín/**29**/15
magazine rack /mǽgəzin-ræk/**29**/14
magnet /mǽgnət/**19**/19
magnifying-glass /mǽgnɪfaɪɪŋ-glæs/**16**/10
mailbag /mél-bæg/**22**/6
mailbox /mél-baks/**14**/1; **22**/4
mailman /mél-mæn/**22**/5
mail slot /mél-slat/**28**/2
mallet /mǽlət/**25**/1
mane /men/**36**/26; **57**/17
mango /mǽŋgo/**61**/15
mantel /mǽntəl/**29**/5
mantis /mǽntɪs/**59**/15
map /mæp/**5**; **18**/19
mascara /mæskǽrə/**12**/13
mask /mæsk/**35**/15
mast /mæst/**43**/3
mat /mæt/**28**/6
match /mæč/**51**/6
match book /mǽč-baks/**51**/5
material /mətíriəl/**53**/13
mattress /mǽtrɪs/**32**/8
meadow /médo/**34**/11
measurement /méžərmənt/**69**
meat /mit/**20**/13
mechanic /məkǽnɪk/**54**/5
medical /médɪkəl/**17**
medicine chest /médɪsɪn-čest/**33**/11
Mediterranean Sea /mɛdɪtərénɪən-sí/**6**/22
Mekong /mékɔŋ/**7**/53
men /men/**10**
menu /ményu/**51**/24
messy /mési/**75**/7b
meter /mítər/**19**/4; **40**/23
microphone /maɪkrəfon/**49**/25
microscope /maɪkrəskop/**19**/9
milk /mɪlk/**20**/10
miner /máɪnər/**54**/7
minus /máɪnəs/**69**/17
minute hand /mínɪt-hænd/**70**/1
mirror /mírər/**32**/13; **40**/3
Mississippi /mɪsɪsípi/**7**/45
mitt /mɪt/**48**/7
money order /mə́ni-ɔrdər/**22**/18
monkey /mə́ŋki/**57**/12
monkey wrench /mə́ŋki-renč/**24**/9
Moon /mun/**4**/6
mop /map/**31**/5
mortar /mɔ́rtər/**19**/21
mosquito /məskíto/**59**/20
moth /mɔθ/**59**/26
mother /mə́ðər/**71**/4
mother-in-law /mə́ðər-ɪn-lɔ/**71**/6
motorboat /mótər-bot/**35**/34; **43**/11
motorcycle /mótər-saɪkəl/**14**/16; **39**/20
mountain /máʊntən/**34**/2
mountain peak /máʊntən pik/**34**/3
mountain range /maʊntən-renj/**7**
mouse /máʊs/**56**/18
mouth /máʊθ/**9**/4
mouthpiece /máʊθ-pis/**49**/23
movie theater /múvi-θitər/**50**/17
movies /múviz/**50**
mudguard /mə́d-gard/**40**/10
mug /məg/**51**/3
multiply by /mə́ltɪplaɪ baɪ/**69**/16
muscle /mə́səl/**9**/31
mushroom /mə́šrum/**62**/14
music /myúzɪk/**49**; **49**/12
musician /myuzíšən/**49**/3
mustache /məstǽš/**9**/10

nail /nel/**8**/31; **25**/11
nail-file /nél-faɪl/**12**/11
nail-brush /nél-braš/**33**/20
nail polish /nél-palɪš/**12**/14
napkin /nǽpkɪn/**30**/28; **51**/32
napkin holder /nǽpkɪn-holdər/**30**/29
narrow /nǽro/**75**/1a
national defense /nǽšənəl-dífens/**45**

rat /ræt/**56**/22
rattle /rǽtəl/**32**/30
razor /rézər/**33**/13
razor-blade /rézər-bled/**33**/14
read /rid/**65**/7
reading /rídiŋ/**52**
rear light /rír-láıt/**40**/30
rearview mirror /rır-vyu-mírər/**38**/1
receipt /rısít/**20**/23
receiver /rısívər/**28**/19
receptionist /rısépšənıst/**21**/25
record /rékərd/**29**/21
record jacket /rékərd-jækət/**29**/22
recreation /rɛkrıešən/**46–52**
rectangle /réktæŋgəl/**68**
red cap /réd-kæp/**54**/14
Red Sea /réd-sí/**6**/25
referee /rɛfərí/**46**/10; **47**/3
refinery /rıfáınəri/**37**/13
reflector /rıflɛ́ktər/**40**/20
refrigerator /rıfríjəretər/**30**/5
reindeer /réndır/**56**/11
reins /renz/**46**/4
relationship /rılɛ́šənšıp/**71**
reptile /réptaıl/**59**
reservoir /rézəvwar/**37**/1
restaurant /réstərant/**51**
return address /rıtárn-ǽdrɛs/**22**/12
revolver /rıválvər/**45**/12
rhinoceros /raınásərəs/**57**/25
rib /rıb/**8**/5
ribbon /ríbən/**53**/24
rice /ráıs/**63**/7
ride /ráıd/**65**/8
rifle /ráıfəl/**45**/2
right angle /ráıt-æŋgəl/**68**/14
right end /raıt-ɛ́nd/**47**/12
right fielder /ráıt-fíldər/**48**/17
right guard /raıt-gárd/**47**/14
right halfback /raıt-hǽf-bæk/**47**/9
right lane /raıt-lén/**39**/6
right tackle /raıt-tǽkəl/**47**/13
rind /raınd/**61**/18
ring /ríŋ/**12**/7; **46**/13
river /rívər/**7**; **34**/12
road /rod/**15**/31; **34**/18; **38–40**
robe /rob/**16**/24
rock /rak/**35**/29
rocket /rákət/**4**/16
Rockies /rákiz/**7**/36
rod /rad/**48**/19
roll /rol/**73**/12
roller /rólər/**12**/22; **24**/15
roll of film /ról-əv-fílm/**52**/24
roll of paper /ról-əv-pépər/**73**/12
roof /ruf/**26**/1
rook /ruk/**52**/4
rooster /rústər/**36**/34
root /rut/**63**/11
rope /rop/**46**/14
rose /roz/**62**/19
rostrum /rástrəm/**49**/13
rotor /rótər/**44**/16
rough /rəf/**75**/4b, 5a
row /rol/**72**/14
row of houses /ró-əv-háuzız/**72**/14
rowboat /ró-bot/**43**/6
rubber boot /rábər-bút/**10**/12
rubber tubing /rábər-túbiŋ/**19**/14
rudder /rádər/**43**/4
ruffle /rəfəl/**53**/14
rug /rəg/**28**/8; **32**/17
ruler /rúlər/**18**/10
run /rən/**65**/9
rung /rəŋ/**23**/6
runway /rʌ́nwe/**44**/19

sack /sæk/**20**/6; **67**/2
sad /sæd/**72**/11b
saddle /sǽdəl/**36**/28; **46**/3
saddlebag /sǽdəl-bæg/**40**/8, 34
safety belt /séfti-bɛlt/**38**/24
safety pin /séfti-pın/**53**/10
Sahara /səhɛ́rə/**7**/41
sail /sel/**43**/2; **65**/10
sailboat /sél-bot/**43**/1
sailor /sélər/**55**/15

salesman /sélzmən/**55**/9
salmon /sǽmən/**58**/4
saltshaker /sɔ́lt-šekər/**30**/39; **51**/28
sand /sænd/**23**/15; **35**/22
sandal /sǽndəl/**13**/17
sandcastle /sǽnd-kæsəl/**35**/23
sandpaper /sǽnd-pepər/**24**/3
sandwich bag /sǽnwıč-bæg/**67**/4
satellite /sǽtəlaıt/**4**/18
saw /sɔ/**25**/17
saxophone /sǽksıfon/**49**/22
scaffolding /skǽfəldıŋ/**23**/7
scale /skel/**22**/2; **33**/24; **59**/7
scales /skelz/**19**/1; **58**/9
scarecrow /skǽr-kro/**36**/13
scarf /skarf/**11**/19
schedule /skéjəl/**41**/15
school /skul/**18**
science /sáıəns/**19**
scissors /sízərz/**53**/26
scooter /skútər/**40**/29
scoreboard /skɔr-bɔ́rd/**47**/23
scorpion /skɔ́rpiən/**58**/27
scouring powder /skáurıŋ-paudər/**31**/9
screen /skrin/**50**/18; **52**/27
screw /skru/**24**/7
screwdriver /skrú-draıvər/**24**/7
scrub brush /skráb-brəš/**31**/10
sea /si/**6–7**; **35**
seagull /sí-gəl/**60**/21
Sea of Japan /sí-əv-jəpǽn/**7**/33
Sea of Okhotsk /sí-əv-okátsk/**7**/34
seal /sil/**57**/9
seam /sim/**53**/3
seashell /sí-šɛl/**35**/27
seaside /sí-saıd/**35**
seat /sit/**38**/23; **40**/7, 30; **41**/8; **50**/20
seat-belt /sít-belt/**38**/24
seawall /sí-wɔl/**35**/10
seaweed /sí-wid/**35**/37
second hand /sékənd-hænd/**70**/3
second baseman /sɛkənd-bésmən/**48**/11
secretary /sékrətɛri/**21**/22
section /sékšən/**61**/17; **68**/21
sedan /sıdǽn/**38**/37
seed /sid/**62**/28
server /sávər/**48**/25
service /sárvıs/**17**
service line /sárvıs-laın/**48**/26
set /sɛt/**50**/4
sew /so/**65**/11
sewer /súər/**14**/10
sewing /sóıŋ/**53**
sewing machine /sóıŋ-məšin/**53**/1
shallow /šǽlo/**74**/6a
shape /šep/**68**
shark /šark/**58**/1
sharp /šarp/**74**/2b
shaving brush /šévıŋ-brəš/**33**/16
shaving mug /šévıŋ-məg/**33**/15
shed /šɛd/**26**/20; **27**/26
sheep /šip/**36**/29
sheet /šit/**32**/5
sheet music /šit-myuzık/**49**/12
shelf /šɛlf/**20**/15; **24**/18; **29**/17; **30**/16
shell /šɛl/**45**/7; **58**/14; **59**/5
shingle /šıŋgəl/**23**/4
ship /šıp/**42**/7
shirt /šərt/**11**/1; **13**/15
shoe /šu/**10**/11; **11**/8
shoelace /šú-les/**11**/9
shoot /šut/**65**/12
shopping bag /šápıŋ-bæg/**67**/18
shopping basket /šápıŋ-bæskıt/**20**/7
shopping cart /šápıŋ-kart/**20**/1
short /šɔrt/**74**/16b
shorts /šɔrts/**10**/5
shortstop /šɔ́rt-stap/**48**/12
shoulder /šóldər/**8**/13
shoulder bag /šóldər-bæg/**13**/4
shoulder-blade /šóldər-bled/**8**/3
shovel /šávəl/**23**/13; **35**/25
shower curtain. /šáuər-kərtən/**33**/31
shower head /šáuər-hɛd/**33**/4
shut /šət/**65**/13; **74**/4a
shutter /šátər/**26**/12
side /sáıd/**68**/13; **69**/5
sidewalk /sáıd-wɔk/**15**/26
siding /sáıdıŋ/**41**/30

signal /sígnəl/**41**/27
signal box /sígnəl-baks/**41**/23
signalman /sígnəlmən/**41**/22
sill /sıl/**26**/11
sing /sıŋ/**65**/14
singer /síŋər/**49**/24
sink /sıŋk/**30**/7; **33**/12
sister /sístər/**71**/5
sister-in-law /sístər-in-lɔ/**71**/8
sit /sıt/**65**/15
site /sáıt/**23**
sixteenth /sıkstínθ/**70**/11
skate /sket/**47**/31
skater /sketər/**47**/30
skeleton /skɛ́lətən/**8**
ski /ski/**47**/26
skier /skíər/**47**/25
skillet /skílıt/**30**/14
skin /skın/**61**/3
ski-pole /skí-pol/**47**/27
skirt /skərt/**13**/8
skull /skəl/**8**/1
sky /skáı/**27**/10
slacks /slæks/**10**/8; **11**/29
sleep /slip/**66**/19
sleeper /slípər/**32**/27
sleeping bag /slípıŋ-bæg/**35**/3
sleeve /sliv/**11**/7
slide /sláıd/**19**/11; **49**/21; **52**/30
slide projector /sláıd-
prəjektər/**52**/29
slide rule /sláıd-rul/**18**/16
sling /slıŋ/**17**/23
slip /slıp/**12**/2
slipper /slípər/**10**/3; **12**/6
sloppy /slápi/**75**/7b
slow /slo/**74**/9b
slug /sləg/**58**/19
small /smɔl/**74**/1b
smile /smaıl/**65**/16
smoke /smok/**17**/13
smokestack /smók-stæk/**37**/7; **42**/9; **43**/21
smooth /smuð/**75**/5b
snail /snel/**58**/13
snake /snek/**59**/6
snap /snæp/**53**/27
sneaker /sníkər/**10**/13
snorkel /snɔ́rkəl/**35**/16
snout /snáut/**56**/4; **58**/8
snow /sno/**27**/5
snowball /snó-bɔl/**27**/6
snowman /snó-mæn/**27**/7
soap /sop/**33**/27
soap powder /sóp-paudər/**20**/28; **31**/18
sock /sak/**10**/6; **13**/12
socket /sákıt/**31**/16
sofa /sófə/**29**/9
soft /sɔft/**74**/13a; **75**/13b
softdrink /sɔ́ft-dríŋk/**51**/13
soldier /sóljər/**45**/1; **55**/12
sole /sol/**9**/40; **11**/10
solid /sálıd/**75**/14a
solid figures /sálıd-fígyərz/**68**
son /sən/**71**/3
son-in-law /sán-ın-lɔ/**71**/7
south /sauθ/**5**/16
South America /sauθ-əmérıkə/**6**/2
South Atlantic /sauθ-ətlǽntık/**6**/12
South China Sea /sáuθ-čaınə-sí/**7**/31
southeast /sáuθ-íst/**5**/16
Southern /sáðərn/**6**/14
South Pacific /sauθ-pəsífık/**6**/10
South Pole /sáuθ-pól/**5**/7
southwest /sáuθ-wést/**5**/16
space /spes/**4**
space-capsule /spés-kæpsəl/**4**/19
spacesuit /spés-sut/**4**/21
space-travel /spés-trævəl/**4**
spark plug /spárk-pləg/**38**/35
sparrow /spǽro/**60**/28
speaker /spíkər/**29**/20; **49**/28
speedometer /spidámətər/**38**/16
spider /spáıdər/**58**/25
spider web /spáıdər-wɛb/**58**/26
spin /spın/**66**/16
spine /spáın/**8**/6; **52**/18
spiral /spáırəl/**68**/1
spoke /spok/**40**/12
sponge /spənj/**33**/26

spool of thread /spul/(/əv θréd/) 53/8; 73/9
spoon /spun/30/32
sport /spɔrt/46–48
sportcoat /spɔ́rt-kot/10/7; 11/27
sports car /spɔ́rts-kar/39/18
sports coupe /spɔ́rts-kup/38/39
spotlight /spát-laɪt/50/7
sprocket /sprákɪt/40/19
square /skwær/68
squash /skwaš/62/7
squirrel /skwɔ́rəl/56/19
stadium /stédiəm/47
stage /stej/50/1
stair /ster/28/11
staircase /stérkes /28/12
stalk /stɔk/61/2; 62/2
stamp /stæmp/22/9
stand /stænd/47/5; 52/28; 65/17
stapler /stéplər/21/7
star /star/4/5
starter /stártər/40/36
station /stéšən/41/13
station wagon /stešən-wægən/38/40
stein /staɪn/51/3
steering wheel /stírɪŋ-hwil/38/17
stem /stɛm/62/23
stenographer /stənɔ́grəfər/16/25
steno pad /sténo-pæ/21/23
stern /stɜrn/43/14
stethoscope /stéθəskop/17/22
steward /stúərd/44/8
stewardess /stúərdəs/44/7
stick /stɪk/46/18
stir /stɜr/65/18
stirrup /stɜ́rəp/46/7
stitch /stɪč/53/17
stomach /stámək/8/17
stone /ston/61/8, 20
stool /stul/19/8; 32/12; 49/18; 51/21
storage tank /stɔ́rɪj-tæŋk/37/14
store /stɔr/15/20
storm cloud /stɔ́rm-klaud/27/2
stove /stov/30/1
straight /stret/74/5b
straight line /strét-láɪn/68/2
straight pin /strét-pɪn/53/12
straw /strɔ/51/12
strawberry /strɔ́beri/61/21
stream /strim/34/7
street /strit/15/31
street light /strít-laɪt/15/22
street sign /strít-saɪn/14/7
string /strɪŋ/22/20; 49/5; 72/8
string of beads /strɪ́ŋ-əv-bídz/72/8
strong /strɔŋ/75/6a
student /stúdənt/18/5
stuffed animal /stáft-ǽnɪməl/32/29
submarine /sábmərin/45/19
subway station /sábwe-stešən/14/3
sugar cane /šúgər-ken/63/9
sugar-bowl /šúgər-bol/30/38
suit /sut/11/6; 13/5
suit jacket /sút jə́kɪt/13//
suitcase /sút-kes/67/19
sun /sən/4/8; 27/9
sun-bather /sɔ́n-beðər/35/13
sunfish /sɔ́n-fɪš/58/15
sunflower /sɔ́n-flauər/62/27
supermarket /súpər-markɪt/20
surf /sɜrf/35/32
swallow /swálo/60/22
swan /swan/60/17
swarm /swɔrm/72/16
swarm of bees /swɔ́rm-əv-bíz/72/16
sweater /swétər/10/9, 15; 13/16
sweep /swip/65/19
swim /swɪm/65/20
swimmer /swímər/35/35
switch /swɪč/28/17; 31/17; 41/26
switchboard /swíč-bɔrd/21/15
swordfish /sɔ́rd-fɪš/58/3

T-formation /tí-fɔrmešən/47/19
T-shirt /tí-šərt/10/4
table /tébəl/30/26; 46/21
table-cloth /tébəl-klɔθ/51/31
table-tennis /tébəl-tɛnɪs/46
tail /tel/44/13; 56/23; 57/2; 58/7
tail fin /tél-fɪn/44/13

taillight /tél-laɪt/38/4
tank /tæŋk/45/8
tanker /tǽŋkər/43/18
tap /tæp/51/20
tape /tep/53/4
tape measure /tép-mežər/53/25
Tasman Sea /tǽzmən-sí/6/30
taxi /tǽksi/14/4
taxicab /tǽksi-kæb/14/4; 40/22
taxi driver /tǽksi-draɪvər/40/25
taxi stand /tǽksi-stænd/40/21
tea /ti/63/8
teacher /tíčər/18/1; 55/11
tea kettle /tí-kɛtəl/30/17
team /tím/72/15
team of players /tím-əv-pléərz/72/15
tear /tɪr/65/21
telegram /téləgræm/22/17
telephone /téləfɔn/21/2; 28/18
telephone book /téləfɔn-buk/28/22
telephone-booth /téləfɔn-buθ/15/28
television /téləvɪžən/29/29
temperature /tempəčur/70
temple /tɛmpəl/9/7
tennis /ténɪs/48
tennis ball /ténɪs-bɔl/48/28
tennis court /ténɪs-kɔrt/48/23
tennis racket /ténɪs-rækɪt/48/27
tennis shoe /tɛnɪs-šu/10/13
tent /tɛnt/35/1
tentacle /téntəkəl/58/24
test tube /tést-tub/19/22
text /tɛkst/52/1
theater /θiétər/50A/; 50/8
thermometer /θərmámɪtər/70/12
thermos /θɜ́rməs/67/9
thick /θɪk/75/15a
thigh /θái/8/33
thimble /θɪmbəl/53/5
thin /θɪn/74/10b; 75/15b
third /θərd/69/13
third baseman /θərd-bésmən/48/13
thread /θred/25/10; 53/8
throat /θrot/8/12
through /θru/76/2
throw /θro/66/9
thruway /θrúwe/39/1
thumb /θəm/8/29
ticket /tíkɪt/41/7
ticket office /tíkɪt-ɔfɪs/41/14
tie /táɪ/11/4; 65/23
ties /tɔ́ɪz/41/25
tiger /táɪgər/57/19
tight /táɪt/75/16b
tile /táɪl/33/29
time /táɪm/70
tire /táɪr/38/8; 40/11
to /tu/77/4
toaster /tóstər/30/18
toboggan /təbágən/47/29
tobogganist /təbágənɪst/47/28
toe /to/9/41
toilet /tɔ́ɪlɪt/33/8
toilet-paper /tɔ́ɪlɪt pepər/33/10
tomato /təméto/62/15
tongue /təŋ/9/14; 59/8
tool /tul/25
tool shed /túl-šed/26/20
tooth /tuθ/9/12
toothbrush /túθ-brəš/33/17
toothpaste /túθ-pest/33/21
top /tap/69/1
torpedo /tɔrpído/45/17
tortoise /tɔ́rtəs/59/2
touch /təč/65/22
toward /tord/77/10
towel /táuəl/33/22; 35/14
towel rack /táuəl-ræk/33/23
toy /tɔ́ɪ/32/19
toybox /tɔ́ɪ-baks/32/18
track /træk/41/24
tractor /trǽktər/36/18
traffic-light /trǽfɪk-laɪt/14/6
trailer /trélər/39/13, 21
trailer truck /trélər-trək/39/11
train /tren/41/1
train station /trén-stešən/41/13
transporter /trǽnzpɔrtər/39/12
trash can /trǽs-kæn/15/27; 67/12

travel /trǽvəl/38–44
trawler /trɔlər/43/17
tree /tri/27/11; 34/15
trenchcoat /trénč-kot/11/12
triangle /tráɪæŋgəl/68
trigger /trígər/45/13
tripod /tráɪpad/19/13
trombone /trambón/49/20
Tropic of Cancer /trápɪk-əv-kǽnsər/5/3
Tropic of Capricorn /trápɪk-əv/ kǽprɪkɔrn/5/5
trousers /trauzərz/11/17
trowel /tráuəl/23/17
truck /trək/14/14; 39/14
truck driver /trók-draɪvər/54/12
trumpet /trómpət/49/19
trunk /trəŋk/27/12; 38/2; 57/22; 63/12; 67/16
trunks /trəŋks/35/20
tub /təb/33/1
tube /tub/73/13
tube of toothpaste /túb-əv-túθ-pest/73/13
tulip /túlɪp/62/22
turkey /tɔ́rki/60/16
turn /tɜrn/66/10
turn signal /tɔ́rn-sɪgnəl/38/5
turntable /tɔ́rn-tebəl/29/19
turtle /tɔ́rtəl/59/4
turtleneck sweater /tɔ́rtəl nɛk swétər/13/1
tusk /təsk/57/23
TV /tí-ví/29/28
twig /twɪg/27/14; 63/14
type /táɪp/66/21
typewriter /táɪp-raɪtər/21/21
typist /táɪpɪst/54/9

ugly /ógli/75/9b
umbrella /əmbrélə/11/24
umpire /ómpaɪər/48/3
uncle /óŋkəl/71/10
under /óndər/76/17
underneath /əndərníθ/76/17
underpass /óndər-pæs/39/3
undershirt /óndər-šərt/10/4
(under)shorts /óndər-šorts/10/5
uniform /yúnifɔrm/16/3
universe /yúnɪvərs/4
up /əp/76/5
upper arm /ópər-árm/8/22
upstairs /əpstérz/28/14
Urals /yúrəlz/7/39
usher /óšər/50/19

vacuum cleaner /vǽkyum-klinər/31/1
valley /vǽli/34/6
valve /vælv/40/13; 49/2
van /væn/14/13; 39/22
vegetables /véjtəbəlz/20/18; 62
vein /ven/9/29
verb /vərb/64–66
vest /vɛst/11/5
village /vílɪj/34/16
vine /váɪn/61/13
viola /vióló/49/7
violin /vaɪəlín/49/4
vise /váɪs/24/8
vulture /vólčər/60/10

waist /west/8/16
waiter /wétər/51/22
waiting room /wétɪŋ-rum/41/18
waitress /wétrəs/54/11
walk /wɔk/65/24
wall /wɔl/26/3; 29/2
wallet /wálɪt/67/21
walnut /wólnət/61/27
warehouse /wǽr-haus/42/3
warship /wɔr-šɪp/45/16
wash /wɔš/65/25
wash cloth /wɔš-klɔθ/33/19
washer /wɔšər/25/12
washing machine /wɔ́šɪŋ-məšín/31/4
wasp /wasp/59/22
wastepaper basket /wés-pepər-bæskɪt/21/13
watch /wač/11/21
watchband /wáč-bænd/11/22
water /wótər/35/31, 42–43
waterfall /wótər-fɔl/34/4
watering-can /wótərɪŋ-kæn/27/23

waterlily /wɔ́tərlɪli/**62**/26
wave /wev/**35**/33; **66**/1
wavy line /wévi-láɪn/**68**/7
weak /wik/**75**/6b
weather /wéðər/**27**
web /wɛb/**58**/26
webbed foot /wɛ́bd-fút/**60**/9
weep /wip/**64**/7
weight /we/**19**/3
west /wɛst/**5**/16
wet /wɛt/**74**/7a
whale /hwel/**57**/1
wharf /wɔrf/**42**/5
wheat /hwit/**36**/14; **63**/2
wheel /hwil/**40**/9
wheelbarrow /hwíl-bæro/**23**/24; **27**/27
whisker /hwískər/**56**/21
whistle /hwísəl/**41**/12
wide /wáɪd/**75**/1b
width /wɪdθ/**69**/8
wife /wáɪf/**71**/1
willow /wílo/**63**/24

wind /wind/**66**/3
windbreaker /wínd-brekər/**35**/18
windlass /wídləs/**42**/16
window /wíndo/**26**/8
window box /wíndo-baks/**26**/13
window frame /wíndo-frem/**26**/9
window pane /wíndo-pen/**26**/10
windowsill /wíndo-sɪl/**26**/11
windpipe /wínd-paɪp/**9**/22
windshield /wín-šild/**38**/10
windshield wiper /wín-šild-waɪpər/**38**/11
wine glass /wáɪn-glæs/**51**/27
wing /wɪŋ/**44**/11; **60**/23
wings /wɪŋz/**50**/5
winter sports /wíntər-spɔ́rts/**47**
witness /wítnɪs/**16**/19
witness stand /wítnɪs-stænd/**16**/18
wolf /wʊlf/**57**/11
women /wímɪn/**12–13**
wood /wʊd/**34**/8
wool /wʊl/**53**/19
workbench /wɔ́rk-bɛnč/**24**/1

workman /wɔ́rkmən/**23**/14
workshop /wɔ́rk-šap/**24**
world /wərld/**5–7**
worm /wərm/**58**/21
wrench /rɛnč/**24**/13
wrestler /réslər/**46**/22
wrestling /réslɪŋ/**46**
wrist /rɪst/**8**/25
write /ráɪt/**66**/2

x-ray /ɛ́ks-re/**17**/24

Yangtze /yǽŋ-tsí/**7**/55
yard /yard/**27**; **80**
Yellow River /yélo-rívər/**7**/54
young /yəŋ/**75**/2a

zebra /zíbrə/**57**/24
zigzag /zíg-zæg/**68**/6
zip code /zíp-kod/**22**/13
zipper /zípər/**53**/22

INDEX FRANÇAIS